Realizing the College Dream with Autism or Asperger Syndrome

also by Ann Palmer

Parenting Across the Autism Spectrum
Unexpected Lessons We've Learned
Maureen Morrell and Ann Palmer
ISBN 1 84310 807 0

of related interest

Succeeding in College with Asperger Syndrome
A student guide
John Harpur, Maria Lawlor and Michael Fitzgerald
ISBN 1 84310 201 3

The Autism Spectrum and Further Education
A Guide to Good Practice
Christine Breakey
ISBN 1 84310 382 6

Employment for Individuals with Asperger Syndrome
or Non-Verbal Learning Disability
Stories and Strategies
Yvona Fast and others
ISBN 1 84310 766 X

How to Find Work that Works for People
with Asperger Syndrome
The Ultimate Guide for Getting People with Asperger Syndrome
into the Workplace (and keeping them there!)
Gail Hawkins
ISBN 184310 151 3

Asperger's Syndrome
A Guide for Parents and Professionals
Tony Attwood
Foreword by Lorna Wing
ISBN 1 85302 577 1

Pretending to be Normal
Living with Asperger's Syndrome
Liane Holliday Willey
Foreword by Tony Attwood
ISBN 1 85302 749 9

Realizing the College Dream with Autism or Asperger Syndrome

A Parent's Guide to Student Success

Ann Palmer

Jessica Kingsley Publishers
London and Philadelphia

First published in 2006
by Jessica Kingsley Publishers
116 Pentonville Road
London N1 9JB, UK
and
400 Market Street, Suite 400
Philadelphia, PA 19106, USA

www.jkp.com

Copyright © Ann Palmer 2006
Second impression 2006
Third impression 2006

Library of Congress Cataloging in Publication Data

Palmer, Ann, 1955-
    Realizing the college dream with autism or Asperger syndrome : a
parent's guide to student success / Ann Palmer. -- 1st American pbk.
ed.
        p. cm.
    Includes bibliographical references and index.
    ISBN-13: 978-1-84310-801-6 (pbk. : alk. paper)
    ISBN-10: 1-84310-801-1 (pbk. : alk. paper)
    1. Asperger's syndrome. 2. Autism. 3. Parents of autistic children.
I. Title.
RC553.A88.P356 2006
616.85'882--dc22

                                        2005023410

British Library Cataloguing in Publication Data
A CIP catalogue record for this book is available from the British Library

ISBN-13: 978 1 84310 801 6
ISBN-10: 1 84310 801 1

Printed and Bound in Great Britain by
Athenaeum Press, Gateshead, Tyne and Wear

I dedicate this book to my family. To my wonderful husband Bobby, thank you for your love, patience, and support. I couldn't have done this without you. To my daughter Sarah and my son Philip, thank you for making me so proud to be your mom. Last but not least to Eric, thank you for everything you have taught me and for all the wonderful people and experiences you have brought to my life. You inspire me every day. Thank you for giving me permission to share your story to inspire others. I love you all.

Acknowledgments

There are many people in Eric's life who have helped him over the years. Without their dedication and hard work and their belief in him, Eric would not be where he is today. I would like to give my heartfelt thanks to Joanna Dalldorf and Lee Marcus for gently giving us the diagnosis and supporting us over the years; to Pat Fennell and Kay Flinn for listening, teaching, and touching our lives in so many ways; to Kim Banks, Artie Cline, Frances Patterson and Anne Murphy, advocates extraordinaire for Eric in school; to Dail Ballard and Linda King-Thomas, therapists who with patience and respect encouraged Eric to try new things; and to Laurie Quartermain and Sabina Vermeulen for helping Eric discover his own voice to advocate for himself.

I also want to thank the friends and colleagues who supported me through the process of writing this book. Thank you to Nancy Huber for helping me get my foot in the door; to Maureen Morrell for encouraging me to do this; to my fellow parents and friends Linda Griffin, Susan Monk, Beth Grunewald, and Elizabeth Ross for sharing their personal feelings about their own children's experiences in college; to the professionals who took the time to answer my many questions, Gladys Williams, Laurie Quartermain, Susan Angle, Jane Warner, and Frances Patterson. Last, to my two best friends, Chris Reagan and Marty Kellogg, for putting up with me and keeping me focused and stress-free; your friendship is my anchor.

Contents

Contents

Preface

After my son Eric was accepted into college word spread in our local autism community that I was the person to call if you had questions about college and autism. I never felt like an expert in this; I was just a mom trying to survive my son leaving home. I was surprised that anyone would be coming to me for advice because I wasn't feeling confident in anything I was doing. That time in my life was very similar to 16 years earlier when Eric was first diagnosed with autism. Like then, I felt overwhelmed, I had more questions than answers, and I was pressuring myself to learn everything and do everything to help my son.

The parents who contacted me, some I knew well and some I had never talked to before, were hungry for information and appreciative of any experience I would share with them. They didn't expect all the answers. They wanted to hear from someone who was going through it, who could talk about the mistakes, the surprises, anything we were learning during this process.

I was very pleased when my colleagues at TEACCH (**T**reatment and **E**ducation of **A**utistic and other **C**ommunication handicapped **CH**ildren and adults) invited me to present at a conference on high-functioning autism and Asperger Syndrome in college. The conference was attended by disability services providers from colleges and universities along the eastern coast of the United States. I was asked to give a parent's perspective and to share some of the strategies that had been useful for Eric. For the first time I would be telling our story to professionals, not parents, and I wasn't sure how well it would be received. I had doubts that an audience of college service providers would be interested in a parent's perspective, knowing the emphasis in college is on student self-advocacy and not parental involvement.

The conference went well and the audience was very receptive to my presentation. I learned that day that college service providers are committed to helping students be successful in college and they welcome a parent's help in preparing the student for the transition and supporting them at college. They understand how complicated the needs of students on the autism spectrum can be. In many cases they alone cannot provide all the supports a student may need and realize that a parent's support may be crucial.

My experience at the conference and the questions I got from other parents convinced me that there is a significant need for more readily available information for professionals and parents who support students on the autism spectrum in college. This book is my attempt to get more information out to other parents who are thinking about college as an option for their child. I hope it will also be helpful to those individuals who work at colleges supporting our sons and daughters. It is my hope that my experiences and the experiences of my son can help other families realize their college dreams.

Introduction

College was never an option. The day the doctor told us that our three-year-old son Eric had autism our world changed forever. Many of the dreams my husband and I had for our son disappeared. My first questions to the doctors were about his future. What would he be like when he is an adult? Will he be able to go to college? Will he ever get married? No one could predict his future and they were unwilling to guess. The doctors would only talk about his strengths and say it was too early to tell. Over time I stopped worrying as much about the future because I was overwhelmed with the present. I had trouble seeing beyond the daily battles and the countless therapy appointments that ruled our lives. My new dreams became very short-term—Eric would be able to sit with the other kids at circle time, Eric would make it through the grocery store that day without a meltdown. I was afraid to hope for more.

Now I know that I was wrong: wrong to give up on dreams for my son and wrong to expect so little. I would have closed many doors if Eric had not reminded me to keep them open by showing me how much he could do. He never let me give up on him. Over time I adjusted to the "autism" and was better able to see his potential. At the same time he began to adjust to his world and to show me his capabilities. He has taught me so much over the last 20 years. The day we moved him into his dormitory room on campus was the proudest moment of my life, and also the scariest.

There were many things to be scared of. For the first time, my son would be on his own, making his own choices, taking care of himself. I wouldn't know what he was doing in his classes, if he were passing or failing, or if his professors understood his difficulties. I had no idea how he would deal with living in a dormitory with loud music and partying late at night. Would sharing a bathroom with six strangers overwhelm him? I didn't know how the other students would treat him or if he would be able to make friends. What if he got sick? What if he needed help? Everything I feared seemed not just possible, but almost certain to happen.

Some of these worries are shared by all parents of children leaving for college for the first time. I recently survived my "severely normal" daughter's transition to college. Although that was hard too, it was different from the experience I had with Eric. As I worried about my daughter's first days and nights at college, I knew deep down that she understood more about life and people and making smart choices, and that she would be OK. Eric, on the other hand, does not have that same level of understanding and probably never will. He may always have trouble seeing another person's perspective and consequently will be more vulnerable. These fears I had were productive because they drove me to try to prepare Eric for what was to come.

Eric's college experience has been at a large state university with close to 30,000 students. That may not be the best environment for all students on the autism spectrum. The sensory issues that many students on the autism spectrum struggle with could make this kind of college environment intolerable. Many students do well at community colleges or smaller schools with more individual attention from instructors, smaller class sizes, and a smaller campus to navigate. Living on campus in a dormitory also may not be the best option for students with autism. Parents need to think about the level of participation that is best for their child, whether it is commuting to classes, attending part-time instead of full-time, or taking online or video classes. The choices Eric made might not be the appropriate choices for your son or daughter. It is important to consider all the options available to your child. You should research the supports colleges offer and weigh each one with your individual child's strengths and needs in mind.

Parents who read this book may not find their own child's experience within these pages. The struggles your son or daughter has may not be the same as the struggles of my son. They may have capabilities Eric does not. I may not have the personal experience of dealing with the same behavior issues or the same social needs that your son or daughter may be experiencing. I include in this book information about other college experiences from a variety of individuals on the autism spectrum. I learned of these college experiences through my conversations with other parents and through my association with professionals in the autism field. Also included are the perspectives of adults on the spectrum who have shared their experiences in college. I hope this book can relate to parents and professionals the wide range of needs and abilities of students on the autism spectrum and the importance of respecting the individuality of each of these students.

I use the word "autism" in this book to describe my son's disability. Autism was the word we were presented with over 18 years ago. It fit then and it fits now. That little word has enabled him to get the services and resources he has needed. It has not held him back in school or in the expectations others have had for him. Perhaps your child has a different diagnosis. Autism spectrum disorder, Asperger Syndrome, high-functioning autism, pervasive developmental disorder, and nonverbal learning disorder are words we often hear describing our children. The names given to our children's disorder may be different, but many of the problems are the same. The experiences described in this book can help families or professionals—basically anyone working with an individual on the autism spectrum who considers higher education an option.

We were fortunate to receive the diagnosis for Eric when he was very young. This gave us many years to adjust, learn, and accept. Many students are being diagnosed with high-functioning autism or Asperger Syndrome later in life. They may have received incorrect diagnoses before finding the one that fits. Many students don't find out they are on the autism spectrum until they are in college. They may have struggled in college and when seeking help found a knowledgeable support person who led them to the answer to their difficulties. Whatever the age of the individual when diagnosed, the supports and strategies that are included in this book can help them and help the family who wants to be a part of the student's support team.

This book is not a story about a child who was "cured" of autism. Yes, my son is able to attend college, live in a dormitory, and be independent in many areas. Obviously, he has succeeded in ways I never could have imagined, but he still has autism and always will. At the age of 22, he prefers being alone. Frequently he self-stims and talks quietly to himself. One of his greatest limitations is his difficulty making friends. He reads constantly, mostly books about dinosaurs, creatures, or evolution, and he has little interest in what anyone else around him may be doing. He needs order in his life and has many routines for his day. The autism is a big part of who he is. What is important is that Eric likes who he is and wouldn't change anything about himself.

One of the best lessons I have learned over the last 20 years is that all individuals on the autism spectrum are different. As a parent of a newly diagnosed son, I searched for that story of the child just like mine and the parent who knew exactly what I was going through. I never found that story, but instead I found things I could identify with in numerous stories of children who were often very different from my son. Those stories helped me more because they taught me about the uniqueness of autism. They reminded me of difficulties I had already survived and problems I would never have to deal with. They gave me hope for the future. It didn't matter as much that the experiences were different from my own. What mattered was that from those stories I felt connections to other people and immediately felt less alone.

I was at the beach with my family recently and a woman approached me while I was sitting in my chair reading. She very nicely said, "I hope you won't think I'm being too personal, but is that your son over there?" Eric was enjoying the beach, running back and forth at the water's edge, occasionally just standing there enjoying the feel of the water on his feet. I said "Yes, that's my son." Even after all these years I worried about what she would say next and readied myself to protect my child. She said, "Does he have autism?" When I answered yes, she quickly said, "My son has autism too," and pointed him out to me in the neighboring group of people on the beach. We struck up a conversation and immediately had a connection that had nothing to do with the functioning level of our children or their ages or what therapy we used. That day on the beach we were strangers who discovered we were members of the same club—not a popular club to join, but a club just the same. Even though our children might be very different, we knew we had paid the same dues to join that club.

For all you fellow autism spectrum club members, I hope you will feel that connection within the pages of this book. My story may not be your story but I know you will understand the fears I have felt, and the dreams I have dreamt. I want this book to give you hope, something I searched for desperately when my son was three. I want our story to remind you not to close any doors because you think your child may not be able to go there. The future is wide open and anything can happen. College doesn't have to be one of the dreams we surrender.

1 Starting Out: Diagnosis and the Early Years

Eric was the perfect baby. He rarely cried. He ate well and he slept well. As a toddler he never got into anything he shouldn't have. He never emptied things out of a cabinet and never climbed on anything. He never colored on the walls or picked up something yucky off the floor and put it in his mouth. He loved to sit in your lap and look at books and could do this for hours. He was enthralled with *Sesame Street*, especially the segments about letters and numbers. At the age of one and a half he was bringing us letter blocks and telling us the letter and then naming something that started with that letter. We thought he must be brilliant.

The phone call came when Eric was two and a half. It was his preschool teacher. She was concerned because Eric wasn't responding when she called his name and he was ignoring the other children in the class. She thought he might have a hearing problem. I knew there was nothing wrong with his hearing. He always covered his ears whenever there was a loud noise. If anything, I thought he had exceptionally good hearing. She must be wrong.

She was wrong about the hearing, but she was right to be concerned. Thanks to that perceptive teacher, we started the process of finding out what was different about Eric. First there was a speech and hearing evaluation ("Have you ever heard of autism?"). Then there was a trip to our pediatrician ("Look at him. He's talking. If he has autism then I'm the Pope!"). Finally there was an evaluation by a developmental pediatrician who kindly told us about our son's autism. The process was painful, but it made us recognize that there was a problem, and we started getting help for Eric. For that I am eternally grateful for that phone call from his preschool teacher.

The grief a parent feels when they find out their child has a disability is different for everyone. For me it was a deep, physical pain deep inside my chest, a weight that was always there. I cried for days until I couldn't cry anymore. I avoided the people who meant the most to me. They wanted to help and wanted to support me but I wasn't able to let them in. I couldn't talk about it and I didn't want anyone to see me so vulnerable. Eventually I realized that I had to take control of my life again. My six-week-old daughter, my husband, and Eric needed me. Fortunately I had the luxury of being a stay-at-home mom and dealt with my grief by focusing on learning more about autism and taking Eric to different therapies. I was also very fortunate to have my family and my husband's family nearby and they helped us physically and emotionally through those early months.

At age three Eric had language and knew many words but he only used his words to name things, mostly in books or on TV. He didn't use his words to communicate with us. He was very echolalic and would repeat back my questions instead of answering yes or no. He could recite the complete dialogue of his favorite video but he couldn't tell me what he wanted. His receptive language was also delayed. He didn't understand much of what people said to him and had difficulty following simple directions.

Socially, Eric was very withdrawn. He was affectionate with his father and me but completely ignored other children and most people around him. He never showed the typical jealousy towards his baby sister and rarely paid any attention to her at all. He was very happy by himself. I used to call it Eric's "phasing out"—when he would look off into the distance and smile and I knew he had left us and was thinking about a book or video he enjoyed. He always had this great ability to block out things that were going on around him. One day during a thunderstorm, our house was struck by lightning. The electricity in half of the house went out, but not in the room where Eric was watching a video. There was no obvious fire, but the firemen were called and they came to check for possible fires smoldering in the attic or in the walls. Here was Eric, watching his video, while numerous large, loud men in full firefighter gear—hats, coats, boots, axes, etc.—marched through the room he was in. Eric completely ignored them. If I hadn't already known something was wrong, I would have definitely known then.

One of the hardest things to deal with in the early years was Eric's routines. He had a routine for eating, getting ready for bed, getting in the car, reading books, for just about everything. If for some reason the routine was interrupted or changed, Eric would get very upset. He would cry non-stop, sometimes for hours. The reasons for his routines weren't often obvious to anyone else. There seemed to be some sort of plan in his head of how things were supposed to happen. When these routines were messed up, I would have no idea what was upsetting him and he couldn't tell me. When Eric was about four years old, we took a ferry ride while at the beach. Soon after the ferry left the dock to start across the bay, Eric became very upset and started screaming "Start over, start over!" Nothing could calm him the whole ride across the bay. In his mind, something happened differently than he expected. Actually he missed the start of the boat moving away from the dock, so he wanted it to start over, like a video. These behaviors were very difficult to deal with, especially in public, and we tried to avoid them whenever we could. During those years our family had very little spontaneity in our lives. We always had to think ahead, how will Eric react to this?

During the first few years following the diagnosis, I felt like we were living in our car. We were on the go constantly to two different preschools, a church preschool for "typical" kids and a Speech and Hearing preschool. We also had speech therapy at our local elementary school, and private occupational therapy and speech therapy once a week. Eric and I also had weekly sessions at Division TEACCH (Treatment and Education of Autistic and other Communication handi-capped CHildren and adults). Eric's therapies and schools were very time-consuming. I was also trying to work with him at home whenever I could. Getting involved in Eric's therapies was my way of coping. In a way it was my own therapy that helped me survive the early years. I needed to feel like I was doing something to help him. I had to have more control over this autism that had invaded our lives.

Elementary school

Our life calmed down quite a bit when Eric started attending public school. He entered a self-contained autism class for elementary school-aged children with high-functioning autism. There were five children, a teacher, and an aide in the classroom. The kids were various ages and Eric, a small five-year-old, was tiny compared to the eight- and nine-year-olds in the class. All the children had some language. They varied quite a bit in their academic abilities and in behaviors.

These were probably the best years of school for Eric. The teacher and aide were both well trained in autism and they obviously cared for the children in the class. Because it was a small class, there were opportunities for one-to-one instruction with the teachers. Social situations were creatively set up in the classroom for the students so they could practice their social skills in a structured environment. The academics were individualized for each student based on their skills and needs. Even though the classroom was not close to my home and I had to transport Eric there each day, it was worth it to have him in this wonderful learning environment.

The teacher spent a great deal of time educating the other teachers and administrators at the school about her students and about autism. She developed a good relationship with the regular education teachers. She would find the ones who wanted her students in their classes and weren't afraid to work with these children. When a student was ready to be mainstreamed into the regular education class, the teacher or aide from the autism class would go with the student. They would gradually spend longer periods of time in the classroom as the student adjusted to it. The autism class teacher would gradually reduce her time in the regular education class, allowing the student to become more independent. By the end of Eric's second year in this class, he was being mainstreamed out successfully for almost half of his school day.

I am often asked by other parents of children with high-functioning autism or Asperger Syndrome about Eric's early experiences in school. I share with them how important the self-contained autism class experience was in preparing Eric for future mainstreaming and inclusion. Frequently parents express their desire for their child to be fully included from the start and not relegated to special education. There is an assumption by many that if our children are in self-contained special education classes the prognosis won't be as good. Students on the autism spectrum do not need to be in regular education classes with "typical" kids to learn and grow. I think it is important to look at each individual child, each individual school and what it has to offer, and to be creative in your place-ment decision for your child. If your son or daughter can be fully included and be successful, that's wonderful. However, some students on the autism spectrum may have difficulties starting school in the often unstructured setting of a large kindergarten class. Some combination of time in a smaller class and time in regular education classes may be more appropriate for these students. A self-contained special education class, with a good teacher who understands autism, can be an option for students with high-functioning autism or Asperger Syndrome. Starting in such a class should not cause the student to lose the opportunity to be in a regular education class in the future.

Unfortunately, our school system decided the cost of this special class for high-functioning kids with autism was too high, and so they ended it. Eric was doing well in the mainstreamed setting, so it was decided he would be fully included in a regular third-grade class at his home school the following school year. This was a huge change for Eric—new school, new big yellow bus, and a new teacher who knew nothing about autism. On the positive side, for the first time Eric would be in his home school with his sister and the children in our neighborhood.

Eric had been fairly sheltered during his years in the self-contained class. Full inclusion was going to bring new issues. I was concerned that other students would notice Eric's differences and might say hurtful things to him or to his sister. We had not told Eric about his autism diag-nosis, and we decided it was now time to talk to him and his sister about it. Eric was seven years old and his sister was five.

Telling your child they have a disability can be very hard. A parent's reluctance to tell their child they have autism or Asperger Syndrome is very understandable. They worry that their child will feel bad about themselves, that their life will be changed forever. Parents may not realize what their children are already sensing and the relief they may feel to know the reason for their differences. As difficult as it may be to tell them, parents should consider the child's right to know.

Knowing when to tell them and what to tell them depends on the child—their ability to understand, their need to know, and the impact it can have on them. Some parents choose to tell their child about their autism when they are very young and others wait until their child is older. Some parents wait until a problem comes up or until the child asks them why they are different or why they don't have any friends. I always think of it as being like the "sex talk." You know it's time to talk to the child when they start asking questions. Then you tell them at the level they can understand at that age. It should be a gradual process, giving them more information as they get older and can understand more. I never expected my first talk with Eric about his autism to be the only talk. I knew his learning about autism and how it affects him would be an ongoing process. Many adults on the autism spectrum have spoken about the issue of when they were told. They often report that they knew they were different even as a young child but didn't know why. Several adults I have heard speak have said it was harder for them growing up without a diagnosis: something that would explain to them why they couldn't seem to fit in.

Of course, many individuals with high-functioning autism or Asperger Syndrome may not get a diagnosis until they are older. As a young adult or adult they are often painfully aware of their differences and a diagnosis provides an explanation. They may have been through a long list of other diagnoses before getting the one that fits. In these situations, telling them about the diagnosis is not an issue. They are old enough to be involved in the whole evaluation and diagnosis process and, one hopes, are hearing about the diagnosis directly from the physician or psychologist.

Telling Eric and his sister was one of the hardest things I have ever done. I worried about it for a long time before I actually did it, so it was a great relief when it was over and we were all fine. In the talk with Eric and later with Sarah, I concentrated on how everyone is different. I used myself and their father and each of them as examples. I talked about how some people can do some things better than others, pointing out what each of them could do well and what was harder for them. I used the word "autism" when I spoke to both children because they were old enough to understand. I explained that Eric's autism means his brain is wired a little differently and that is why he often prefers to play alone or gets upset sometimes in new situations. After telling them both, I was still worried about the comments they might hear at school, but felt that they were better prepared to deal with them. They also knew that they could come to me and their father and talk about it whenever they had questions.

There were other ways that I tried to prepare Eric for the transition to full inclusion in the third grade. We visited the school during the summer and explored the campus and playground. We talked about how great it would be to have Eric and his sister riding on the same bus to school. We tried to build up the experience and how wonderful it was going to be. Because we were treating it as an adventure, Eric was excited.

Eric's third-grade teacher had been teaching for many years. She was nice and seemed like a good teacher, but it became clear very soon after school started that she was not comfortable having Eric in her class. The notes started coming home: his desk is messy, he doesn't write his math problems on the lines properly. (It didn't matter that he got all the answers correct.) Then there was the phone call one night when she said to me, "Eric is awfully small for his age. Don't you think he would be better off in second grade?" I reminded her that he had already mastered the second-grade curriculum and third grade was where he should be.

I tried to understand her concerns but it was hard. Eric was probably her easiest student. He always followed the rules, he never talked in class or disrupted the class in any way, and he always did the work required of him. I think the teacher was worried about what Eric *might* do. After five months of my trying to convince her that Eric was not going to suddenly flip out in her class, she called me at home one night. She had watched a television show on facilitated communication that featured several severely autistic children. She was moved by the show and said to me, "Eric is doing really quite well, isn't he?" After almost five months of trying to convince her of this same thing, she finally got it. From that point on, the teacher was more understanding and supportive. She actually became so supportive and protective that she didn't want Eric to fail at anything. I had to remind her to challenge him and to let him try new things even if he failed.

The primary support for Eric during his years of inclusion in regular education was the autism outreach teacher from our school system. This person's responsibility was to support those students on the autism spectrum who were not in autism-specific classrooms. The students could be in other special education classrooms or in regular education classrooms. This teacher was available to provide information about autism to the teachers and to the other children in the class if needed.

For the first two years of full inclusion, Eric's autism outreach teacher was his former teacher in the self-contained autism class. When they disbanded the class, she became the outreach teacher. It was wonderful to have her to help Eric through this transition to full inclusion. She knew him well and she was very knowledgeable about autism. She was also an excellent ambassador to the regular education teachers. She could go into the classroom and set up schedules or organizational help for the students. She could also work with the students one-to-one occasionally if they needed the extra help with academics. The level of support she provided was individualized for each student depending on their needs. For Eric, she primarily offered support to the teachers and education about the autism spectrum and about Eric's individual needs. She went into the classroom once a week to work with Eric on some of the academic work. She also came to the class once a week to help facilitate social experiences for Eric on the playground.

Before her change of heart, Eric's third-grade teacher was not happy about what Eric did on the playground. Instead of playing with the other children, he would walk back and forth and quietly talk to himself. He was very happy when he did this and I felt that he needed this time to himself during recess. In my opinion he was doing a great job focusing in the classroom and holding himself together. If he wanted to do this during recess because it relaxed him and calmed him, then he should be allowed to do so. When I observed, the other students in the class did not seem to be bothered by Eric's actions—in fact they didn't even seem to notice. But the teacher was not comfortable with this and asked that the autism outreach teacher come and help Eric do something with the other students. She set up a "peer buddy" on the playground once a week whose responsibility was to play with Eric. The little girls that volunteered to do this were great and seemed to enjoy the challenge of getting Eric to connect.

Our first autism outreach teacher left the school system after Eric's fourth-grade year. It was hard to see her go. She had been so important to Eric and to me. Fortunately, the person who took her place was also wonderful. He was trained and experienced in the field of autism and worked well with the regular education teachers. He was a resource for Eric throughout the remaining years of public school. Eric no longer needed one-to-one support in the classroom. The new outreach teacher's primary support for Eric was to consult to and meet with Eric's teachers on a regular basis. He also attended all the Individualized Educational Plan (IEP) meetings.

In addition to helping Eric, the outreach teacher was a support for me personally. Here was someone I didn't have to educate about my son. He already knew the uniqueness of these students and nothing surprised him. He helped me to see some of Eric's strengths that I hadn't been able to see. He also served as a go-between for me with the teachers. If Eric were getting bad grades or if I were seeing problems Eric was having in the classroom, I would call the outreach teacher. He would then contact the teacher to discuss how things were going and offer solutions. The teachers could talk about their frustrations or whatever with the outreach teacher, something they would not feel comfortable doing with a parent. Teachers also seemed to respond better to suggestions from another teacher with experience working with these students than they did to a parent's suggestions. My relationships with Eric's teachers over the years were less complicated because of the support of the outreach teacher. At difficult IEP meetings, the outreach teacher was extremely helpful. There were several times over the years that he would help me defend Eric's need for services when the school would try to remove supports. He helped the other members of the team understand that Eric was doing well because of the supports and that to take them away would be a mistake.

Eric continued with inclusion throughout the remainder of elementary school with very few significant problems. The teachers and the principal were supportive most of the time. School was not easy for Eric and he didn't enjoy going to school. He had to work hard to hold it together during the day. The numbers of kids in the class and the noise and activity levels were difficult for him to handle sometimes. Luckily, the academics were fairly easy for Eric overall but his writing was very slow and made it hard for him to keep up. Homework was long and tedious and Eric had problems getting himself organized. He required one-to-one help at home with most assignments.

As the years went by the people at the elementary school, the teachers and the students learned more about autism and came to understand Eric and accept him for who he was. It helped that the students in his class were told about his autism each year. This is a very personal decision that must be made carefully and with the approval of the person with autism. It may not be the right choice for all students on the autism spectrum. We discussed it with Eric and explained why we thought it would be helpful. He agreed that the other students should be told. We knew Eric's behaviors would set him apart from the other students and that they would know something was different. When they understood it was the autism that made it difficult for him to communicate or made him act oddly at times, they were much more patient and supportive.

The autism outreach teacher talked to the class about Eric's autism each year. (Eric was out of the classroom during these discussions.) He did a great job explaining the autism at the level the students could understand. He talked about it in much the same way as I did when explaining the diagnosis to Eric. He talked about how all children have differences and some can do things better than others and that everyone can do something well. He had the students talk about what they did well and what they had trouble doing. He then asked them to share what things they had seen Eric do well. The students had the opportunity to ask questions about autism and about Eric's behaviors. Eric had very few bullying experiences in elementary school and I think educating the students had a great deal to do with that.

Middle school

I began worrying about middle school when Eric was in the third grade. I had heard and read other parents' stories about bullying and social problems in middle school. I dreaded leaving the smaller, intimate campus of his elementary school where everyone had known him for years. I knew everything would be harder for Eric and that he would need as much preparation as possible for the transition.

I have a very vivid imagination. The picture in my mind of middle school was of total chaos, constant bullying, flunking classes, and Eric wandering the halls lost in a sea of students. Middle school was not like that. There were only a few bullying episodes. Eric never flunked any classes, and he learned to navigate the large campus fairly easily. This is not to say there weren't problems, because there were. Middle school brought what were definitely the hardest years of public school for Eric and for me as his mother. But we both survived the three years of middle school relatively unscathed and those years actually turned out to be good learning experiences for both of us.

Preparation for the transition to middle school was important. It began in elementary school, in the fourth grade, well before the actual transition. When we had Eric's IEP meeting at the end of fourth grade, our focus was on the skills he would need for middle school. We wanted to work on these skills during his last year of elementary school. We included goals in the IEP that targeted independence, social skills, and organizational skills (skills he would also eventually need in college). I knew these were weak areas for Eric and could be problems for him in middle school.

In addition to preparing Eric, I also needed to prepare myself for the transition by learning as much as I could about middle school. I talked to other parents of children on the autism spectrum who had been through middle school to find out what was helpful. I talked to friends with "typical" middle school children about what the student needs to be able to do in middle school. I called the guidance counselor at the middle school and asked her questions about the middle school student's responsibilities. She explained about the "team" teaching concept used in our middle school and the role the guidance counselor would play when Eric came to her school.

At the end of fifth grade, when the transition to middle school was looming ahead of us, we had a very important IEP meeting. I requested the meeting to take place at the middle school, not at the elementary school where it would normally have occurred. I also invited everyone I could think of who could be helpful to us during this transition. The expected members of the team were there: the autism outreach teacher, the exceptional children's (EC) representative from the elementary school and the EC representative from the middle school, the principal of the elementary school, the occupational therapist from the school system, and Eric's current elementary school teacher. We also invited a middle school teacher to attend, someone who knew the sixth-grade curriculum. Eric's sixth-grade teacher had not been chosen yet, or they would have been included. The guidance counselor from the middle school was also there. It was necessary to get the people who had worked with Eric in elementary school together with the people who were going to support him in middle school. The information that was shared during the meeting was crucial to Eric's smooth transition to middle school.

Middle school meant there would be many changes, and change was not easy for Eric. At this age he was less rigid about his routines than he had been, but I knew he still needed time to prepare for the newness of everything he would be facing. Over the summer before middle school we talked about his new school quite a bit and drove by the school, pointing it out to him. Visits to the school were also helpful and we went there several times during the summer to familiarize Eric with the campus. I also arranged for Eric to get a copy of his class schedule early. We were able to walk through his schedule at the school ahead of time. The Open House, when students would normally walk their schedules for the first time with their parents, is usually loud, crowded, and confusing. I knew that would be overwhelming for Eric and not a good environment for him to learn his route to classes. We attended Open House, but after we had already walked his schedule at a quieter time.

The success of a student on the autism spectrum in middle school can be dependent on the amount and quality of communication between the school and home. Unfortunately, parents often find it harder to communicate with teachers in middle school and high school than with those in elementary school. Communicating the needs of your child to seven teachers is difficult. At many middle schools each teacher may have over one hundred different students a day. Daily communications or even weekly communications home are usually impossible.

It becomes more important than ever to meet with as many of the teachers as possible before the school year begins. When I met with the middle school teachers before school started I shared my concerns for Eric. I described what I thought would be difficult for him, and what information I would like teachers to relay to me about his progress or difficulties. I also emphasized to them that I was willing to support them in any way I could. If they wanted more information about autism or about Eric, I would be happy to try to answer their questions. I also volunteered to help in the classroom or on field trips. Meetings like this with parents before the start of school also gives teachers the opportunity to ask questions about the student and the disability and voice any concerns they may have.

A large number of people are going to have contact with your child in middle school. It helps to have at least one person at the school who knows your child and is willing to advocate for them. This may be a special education teacher, a guidance counselor, a principal, or a teacher. The guidance counselor was our consistent support person every year of middle school. I also found at least one person on Eric's team of teachers each year who was particularly supportive and was willing to be a contact for me about my child. The teacher of the autism class at the middle school was also a good resource available to the other teachers. Even though she was not directly working with Eric, the teachers could contact her if they had questions about autism or wanted help developing strategies. It can be beneficial to have a student on the autism spectrum included at a school where a self-contained autism class is located. There is frequently more knowledge about autism at the school and the teacher and the classroom can be used as resources for the included student.

Organizational issues are often one of the biggest problems for included students on the autism spectrum in middle school. All teenagers have difficulty in this area to a certain degree, but for these students it can be a much bigger problem. For the first time, Eric was going to be changing classes seven times a day. He would have to keep up with assignments, notebooks, and books from seven different classes. I knew he would need accommodations and strategies to help with the organizational issues he would face in middle school.

The students at our middle school were required to have a small three-ring notebook for each class. Knowing Eric would not be able to keep track of so many notebooks, we requested he use one large notebook for all his classes. We used subject dividers with pockets between each class section. One pocket was designated for things to come home: assignments, notes to parents, etc. One pocket was for things to go to school: homework, notes to teachers, signed permission slips, etc. The notebook also had a clear cover under which we could place a copy of Eric's schedule that would be visible from the outside of the notebook.

Eric's middle school had a very complicated class schedule and no consecutive days had the same time schedule for classes. There were "block" days when certain classes were extended and certain classes were not on the schedule at all. This was going to be a challenge for Eric. To help with this, I made a simple, easy-to-read schedule that included each day of the week and placed it in the cover of his notebook. Each class was color coded on the schedule, green for science, blue for math, etc. so Eric could easily see on the schedule what classes he would have that day. I also included in the schedule possible times when he might go to his locker and to the bathroom if needed. I had to research this a bit, finding out when the classes were located near enough to each other to allow time to go to the locker or bathroom.

If you have ever been in a large middle school when the bell rings between classes, you know how chaotic and loud it is. The halls are suddenly filled with stampeding students, all talking at once, bumping into each other as they hurry to get to class or to their locker. It is very overwhelming, even for people without sensory issues. With all the noise and bedlam going on around them, and having to hurry too, it can be a real challenge for the student to concentrate on what they should be doing. The location of the locker for the student on the autism spectrum is important. We had Eric's locker assigned near a supportive teacher's class-room, someone who didn't mind keeping an eye out for Eric between classes. Frequently, middle school teachers will be asked to stand in the doorway of their classroom between classes to help monitor the halls. You also want the locker located near as many of the student's classes as possible. The time between classes is extremely short and students have to hurry if they want to go by their locker and get to class on time. Our middle school had top and bottom lockers in the hall and we always made sure Eric got a top locker and one on the end of a row. That way he was not crowded by students on both sides of him or above him and could have easier access to the locker.

The lock on the locker can be a problem for the student on the autism spectrum. Our middle school required a standard spin dial combination lock for the locker. With Eric's fine motor delays, this kind of lock was very difficult for him, especially if he had to hurry. We arranged for Eric to use another kind of lock, a roll dial lock where he rolled in the numbers of the combination. As long as the school is given the combination of the lock, my experience is they are usually agreeable to this accommodation.

There are also ways to organize the inside of the locker to help the student. You can buy locker organizers that compartmentalize the locker so the student can find things more easily. We also found it helped to post a schedule inside the locker that told Eric what to put in the locker at each visit and what to remove. For example it might say: "Put in English and math textbook, take out social studies notebook and your lunch." This strategy can be very helpful in the beginning and, as the school year progresses, the student may need less assistance of this type.

In middle school teachers expect more independence from their students. The homework assignments may be written on the board in the classroom each day before class. Students are then expected to take responsibility to write them down in their assignment book without reminders from the teacher. Then students must organize themselves enough to remember to have the correct textbook, notebook, and assignment for each class in their backpack at the end of school. This was very difficult for Eric. Many times when he would get home from school he would have the book and not the notebook, or the assignment and not the book. One helpful solution for us was to have an extra set of textbooks for home. This was included in the modifications in his IEP and saved us many unnecessary trips back to the school to get a forgotten book.

Many of the modifications available to students with learning disabilities are available for autistic students. Our middle school had highlighted textbooks that were prepared by the Parent Teacher Association (PTA) and available for students with learning disabilities. The textbooks would have the key points in each chapter highlighted or underlined. This can be very useful to students who have difficulty determining what the important parts of a chapter are when it is time to study. As I mentioned earlier, in our middle school the students were assigned to "teams" for each grade. Each year we arranged for Eric to be on the team that included the students with learning disabilities. This team had an additional teacher, a learning disabilities resource teacher, who was available to the students on that team. They would go from one class to another to help when needed with testing, special classroom projects, etc. This team of teachers was already prepared to make modifications for the learning disabled students and therefore was more accepting of any modifications Eric might need.

In addition to the organizational issues, the social dynamics of middle school are very complicated and difficult for all teenagers, but especially for students on the autism spectrum. Anyone who can remember their own middle school years can remember the angst a teenager goes through developing friendships during those years. Students in middle school are very sensitive to differences as everyone strives to be like everyone else. For socially withdrawn students such as Eric, totally avoiding social situations may be the answer. Eric didn't mind not having friends or going to parties or the mall. He walked the halls of middle school as one with blinders on, oblivious to the personal relationships and social battles of the teenagers around him. However, other students on the autism spectrum may be very social and want to have friends but struggle with initiating conversations with others. For those students, individual or group therapy that specifically works on social skills can be helpful. There may be appropriate speech, occupational therapy, or autism-related programs in your area that offer social groups. Most public schools do not offer this resource unless they have several included students on the autism spectrum at the school.

Without that resource available from the school, trying to figure out creative ways to work on social skills with Eric within the middle school seemed a waste of time. It was too difficult to find "typical" middle-school-aged kids who were willing to invite him into their world. There were a few students who occasionally helped Eric. But for the most part, it was not a time to look for good role models or students willing to step outside of the group to be friends with someone who was different. I found it more helpful to concentrate on developing social situations for Eric with family and friends outside of school.

During his time in middle school my concerns for Eric were that he would get lost in the shuffle and no one would know if he was being bullied or treated badly by the other students. I was not sure he would be able to defend himself in those situations. Eric had a bad experience in the physical education (PE) class in middle school. I had no idea that things weren't going well until I asked him how his PE class was going and he frowned as he said, "OK." When I asked him why he didn't like his class, he responded that the kids were mean to him there. After further questioning, I discovered that other students were putting their hands on him and being rough with him while in the locker room. After a few minutes of alarm, I made myself calm down enough to call the school and talk to someone about what was happening. We arranged that Eric would not go into the locker room anymore where there was no adult supervision. Although this experience scared me, it taught me that Eric didn't always know what was important to report to someone. It brought about a good talk between Eric and me about safety and dangerous situations and what information the teachers and his parents needed to know.

Despite the difficulties, the three years of middle school were good for Eric. He learned to be more independent, which was critical for success in high school and college. He adapted to crowds of people and hectic schedules. He got used to following a schedule and became more organized in doing his academic work. As a parent, I learned a great deal too. Not only did I learn about my son's needs and vulnerabilities, I learned how much he could do. He surprised me with his flexibility and calmness during a time in his life that could have been very stressful.

Toward the end of middle school, we were still not considering college as an option for Eric. Then one day Eric brought home a sign-up sheet for the courses he would be taking in high school. He was not just choosing courses for the following ninth-grade year, but for all four years of high school. The school needed to know what course of study the students would be on: certificate, college, or vocational. For the first time, we had to consider whether college was possible for Eric. So far, Eric was doing well in his academic courses, but he still required quite a bit of help. Hoping that his successes would continue, we made the decision to keep him in college preparatory classes. I had doubts that he would have the grades or standardized test scores to get into a college but I wanted him to continue to be challenged and accomplish all he could. As it turned out, the high school years were an incredible growth period for Eric, academically and socially, and he was going to surprise me again.

2 Strategies for the High School Years

After surviving the stressful years of middle school, I was hopeful that high school would be easier. The high school Eric would be attending was huge, close to 2000 students. I was worried about the transition to a new school and Eric's ability to navigate the complicated campus. I knew there would be many students at the high school who had never gone to school with Eric before. I wasn't sure how accepting they would be. I didn't know the staff or teachers, didn't know how involved I could be in advocating for Eric. I was told that there had never been an identified student on the autism spectrum fully included at the school. It looked like we were "paving the way" again.

All students with disabilities at our high school are assigned a case manager. Eric's case manager called me at home before the beginning of school. She was a special education teacher working primarily with learning disabled students. She would be available to help Eric if needed, and also be a resource for the teachers if they had questions about autism or any problems in the classroom. She also informed me that she had a personal connection to autism, a young grandson on the spectrum. It was a relief to know that she would be at the high school to advocate for Eric and to help him through the transition to high school. There were a number of times in high school when Eric needed to go to her for help. At the beginning of each school year Eric would often need to go to her classroom when he wasn't sure where he was supposed to be or if he had trouble finding a classroom. If your son or daughter does not have a person assigned to advocate for them at the school, you may be able to find someone on the campus willing to do that for that student. It is also important to find a guidance counselor at the school who can be an advocate for your child. The guidance counselor should have some knowledge about prospective colleges and keep up to date on the various requirements and levels of accommodations that are offered. Connecting with the guidance counselor early in high school can help guide the student through the important process of preparing for the college transition.

Now that we had made the decision to continue on the "college track," the academics became more important than ever before. I knew that Eric's grades from that point on counted. Colleges would be looking at his grade point average as well as the difficulty level of the classes he was taking. After years of having to help Eric so much with schoolwork, it was hard for me to imagine him being independent enough to do the academics of high school, let alone college. Eric proved to me very soon after starting high school that he could do the work required with very little help and do it better than I expected. I was beginning to see Eric's real potential for the first time.

There were several aspects of high school that made things easier for Eric academically. At our particular high school they offered a class called "curriculum enhancement." Most high schools probably have a class like this but may call it something else. The class was taught by a member of the special education staff, usually a learning disability resource teacher. The class was small and students received instruction to help with organizational and study skills. Most of the class-time students worked on homework and assignments from other classes with help from the teacher if needed. This was a great class for Eric and he took it every year of high school as one of his electives.

The variety of classes offered in high school was also helpful to Eric. He had more choices and could take courses that were centered around his interests. Students on the autism spectrum will most likely do better in a class that involves a student's interest or is in an area in which the student is particularly knowledgeable. Our high school had a study program for students wanting to go into the animal science field. The animal science courses Eric took counted toward the required hours of science needed for graduation. Because of his interest in animals, these classes were more meaningful to Eric than other kinds of sciences such as chemistry or physics. It also enabled Eric to be in courses with other students with similar interests.

Unlike at middle school, many required courses in high school have different levels of difficulty. For example, a student can take English at the basic level, at honors level, or at the advanced placement level. Advanced placement is comparable to a college-level class in difficulty and amount of material covered. Having various levels of courses allowed Eric to take the higher-level classes in subjects he excelled in and take the basic-level classes in those areas that were more difficult for him. The higher-level classes also helped prepare Eric for the rigors of college academics. Colleges will be looking at the level of difficulty of the courses the student is taking in high school. Advanced placement courses are going to look good on a student's transcripts to college. Many colleges want to see that a student has followed a rigorous academic schedule, especially during their junior and senior years of high school.

Students on the autism spectrum in high school who are expecting to continue on to college after graduation need to know the courses that will be required to get into college. They should work with the guidance counselor at the high school to make sure they are taking the necessary courses. Students should start as early as the last year of middle school to map out their academic schedule towards graduation. Colleges will vary as to what is required, so students need to research the requirements of any colleges they are considering.

Most colleges and universities require a certain number of years of a foreign language and certain mathematics or science courses. Eric did not take a foreign language in high school. We knew it would be hard for him and he had no interest in foreign languages at all. He took the curriculum enhancement class instead, which he needed in order to do well in his other courses. We later found out that the university he wanted to attend required two years of a foreign language. Fortunately, the university agreed to waive the requirement for admission as long as he took the foreign language while a student at the university. Not all colleges will agree to do that, so students need to plan their high school course schedule with this in mind. Most colleges do not accept course waivers; therefore, courses waived or avoided because of a learning disability may jeopardize college admission. If the student discovers too late that they don't have the required courses for entrance into a particular college, they can look into taking the courses needed at a local community college.

High school students can prepare for college by taking computer courses and becoming more comfortable with using the computer for assignments. Colleges require most papers and assignments to be done on a word processor and students should have some skill in this area if possible. Students who have an easier time typing than handwriting will appreciate this at the college level where very little is handwritten. A student may also want to get some experience in high school with making graphs or tables on the computer. Any online research experience can also be beneficial in high school to prepare the student for college.

PE classes are usually required in high school. The negative experience of the middle school PE class convinced me that it was not appropriate for Eric to take the standard PE class required for graduation. He hated sports and, because of his motor delays, he was lousy at any kind of team sports. Why put him through it? I tried to have him exempted from PE in high school as I had done for the second year of PE in middle school. I was not successful in this endeavor. The high school required Eric to take some kind of PE class for graduation, but it did not have to be the standard course required for freshmen. Again, the variety of high school classes was to our advantage. We found a PE class that involved weight lifting and running, both sports Eric could participate in somewhat independently. The teacher for the class was great, knew nothing about autism, but was open to learning how best to help Eric.

Not all of Eric's teachers were as accommodating in high school, however. For the most part, the teachers were supportive and willing to do the minor accommodations Eric needed. We had one experience with a teacher that was quite difficult. The class was physical science, a required class for graduation. When Eric started having some problems with the homework and had a low test score, I contacted the teacher via e-mail to tell her my concerns and to ask how I could help Eric at home with his work. She didn't respond to my e-mail. I then tried calling her and leaving a message on her school voice-mail and she never responded to that either. Eric's case manager at the school also tried to talk to her with no success. Eric's grades continued to decline and we called a meeting with the teacher and the autism outreach teacher and myself but the teacher did not attend. I was very frustrated at this point because I knew Eric was a good student. He always followed the rules and always did his work. We weren't asking for anything above and beyond what a "typical" student might need.

Eventually it came to our attention that this particular teacher, along with a few other teachers at the school, had been involved in a law suit initiated by parents of several students with learning disabilities. I never met with or talked to the teacher to get her perspective. My assumption is that because of that difficult experience with the law suit, she was refusing to get involved with students with disabilities who needed accommodations. I eventually had Eric taken out of this teacher's class and put in another class. I mention this story for several reasons. First, it is important that parents pick their battles. I could have pursued this further and gone the legal route to get what Eric needed. But this was not a battle I wanted to fight because I didn't think the end result would have made the teacher be more responsive to students with disabilities. Second, it taught me the lesson that we all, professionals and parents, have "baggage" that we bring to a relationship, based on our previous experiences. We have to work hard to not let past experiences cloud our future relationships and how we advocate for these students.

One professional who is important in the transition to college process is the psychologist with the school. If the student is in a private school or is home schooled it will most likely be a psychologist in private practice who will be involved. In preparation for the transition to college, a student with a disability needs to have a complete psycho-educational battery of testing completed before graduation. The information from this evaluation is needed to acquire testing accommodations for the College Board examinations. It is also necessary for requesting accommodations at the college level. Most colleges require recent (i.e. less than three years old) documentation concerning the disability. It is helpful if the student or parents know before the evaluation what testing the college requires for receiving accommodations. That way they can make sure the appropriate testing is done before graduation from high school. The information required by the college may also give the psychologist some guidance as to what information to stress in the written report from the evaluation. If the testing is not done in high school, or if the testing is not current enough for the college, the parents may find it necessary to pay to have the testing done privately. This can be very expensive.

Probably the most important event that will take place during the high school years for any student with a disability is the Transition Plan. In 1990, there were concerns that special education programs in the schools were not adequately preparing students for adult life. The Congress of the United States amended federal law, the Individuals with Disabilities Education Act (IDEA), to require that each student of high school age have a Transition Plan. Students or parents can request a Transition Plan when the student reaches the age of 14 or earlier if appropriate. The goal of transition planning is to determine what services will be provided to the student during the high school years. These should not consist only of a list of agencies that can be resources for the student following graduation. They should address the high school years and focus on ways to educate the student in the skills they will need as an adult (Reiser 1995).

IDEA defines transition services as a "coordinated set of activities for a student that promotes movement from school to post-school activities." These activities can include postsecondary education, vocational training, supported employment or integrated employment, adult education, adult services, independent living, and community participation. These activities must reflect the individual student's needs and preferences and interests (IDEA 1990, section 1401(a)(19)).

The Individualized Transition Plan (ITP) is often developed as a part of the Individualized Educational Plan (IEP) for the student and should be reviewed annually. It includes long-range goals and services and is oriented to life after high school. The importance of the ITP is to clarify what the individual student wants in his or her life. The ITP team should be thinking about what the student wants to be doing in the future, where they want to live, what their dreams are and what they need to learn or do to reach these dreams.

There are many areas that can be addressed in an ITP in addition to the academic issues. Some of the goals written in the Transition Plan may address a specific skill. Goals may also address basic life skills such as the use of money, personal hygiene, transportation, assistive technology, and self-advocacy. The Transition Plan is a wonderful opportunity to concentrate on the individual student and help them to understand their disability and be able to advocate for themselves. Discussion in the ITP should include ways to help the student identify and access support services in the community such as Vocational Rehabilitation (VR), Social Security, or residential support services. In the past, educators have had to provide school-based services only. Now, with transition services, schools must include instructional and educational experiences that may need to occur outside the school campus.

Students with disabilities often learn a needed skill in the classroom and then practice it in the classroom. The next step should be to practice the skill in the community. Some schools may be reluctant to use a community-based approach to teaching the student the skills needed for transition. When turning down a request for community instruction, it is not uncommon for schools to report issues related to staffing, funding, transportation, safety, or liability. Parents and students may need to advocate for more community-based instruction opportunities for the student. This may be necessary especially for those students who are not in self-contained special education classrooms where non-academic skills are more frequently taught. Being in the mainstream setting may mean fewer opportunities to teach self-help and independence skills to the student.

I arranged for Eric to work at a library in the community one period a day during one of his years in high school. It helped him learn some vocational skills that he would not have the chance to learn in the school setting. The school was agreeable but I had to suggest it, I had to arrange it with the library, and I had to transport Eric to the library. VR was involved in supporting him by meeting occasionally with Eric's supervisor at the library. They also paid Eric a small stipend while he worked there. If working in the community is not available to your child, there may be jobs available on campus that can be pursued. Possible jobs may include working in the main office or the guidance office, working in the cafeteria, or working in the mailroom. During the last two years of high school, Eric worked in the high school library one period each day. This was good experience and also gave him the opportunity to meet more students and feel more involved with the school. Parents may need to initiate ideas such as these as schools frequently will not.

Leisure and recreational skills should be included as part of the goals in the ITP related to community participation. All leisure activities and ideas should be based on the individual interests and desires of the student. Specific skills can be developed to enable the student to participate in a recreational activity the student enjoys such as singing, bowling, swimming, etc. Goals also might focus on skills to help the student learn how to choose leisure activities or how to use their leisure time constructively. Ideas for recreational goals may include attending activities and sporting events on the school campus or attending activities in the community.

Personal and social skills should also be addressed in the student's Transition Plan. Good personal and social skills can benefit the student in most areas of their life. Goals should again be based on the individual preferences of the student and should be individualized to meet the student's specific needs. Goals may include learning how to greet people, developing better eye contact, improving table manners, or understanding the difference between strangers and acquaintances. The ITP team, including the student, should assess what the social and personal needs are of the student and develop goals based on that information.

High school was a time of growth for Eric socially as well as academically. For most individuals on the autism spectrum, social skills are going to be an ongoing challenge. As I mentioned before, Eric had always been a loner and not very social with anyone outside of family. He was socially appropriate in most situations; he just didn't like to initiate social contact and often preferred to be alone. Eric became more social in high school as he realized how enjoyable it was to talk to girls. There was one particular girl in one of his classes who was friendly with Eric and invited him to sit with her and her friends at lunch. For the first time in his school career, Eric was not eating lunch alone. She became his friend, inviting him to activities at the school and in the community. Eric's relationship with this girl was a wonderful gift. It gave him confidence and showed him how pleasurable having friends can be.

After the social difficulties of middle school, it was refreshing to have a positive social experience for Eric, especially one that I didn't arrange! Of course social experiences in high school will vary. They may not always be successful and many individuals on the autism spectrum report extremely difficult experiences in high school. However, many parents have told me and I certainly have found that high school is easier socially than middle school. Students in high school may be more accepting of differences than students in middle school.

As parents, the social rejection of our children is one of the most painful things we can experience. For the student, social rejection can be devastating. Individuals on the autism spectrum will probably always have to work hard to deal with the social aspects of their world. But as individuals mature, they learn more about themselves and their strengths and difficulties and, we hope, can adjust better to the social demands they face. As adults, they will also have more social opportunities with people who are more mature and more accepting. I believe social experiences can get better as the individual on the spectrum gets older.

For some individuals on the autism spectrum, the Transition Plan meeting may be their first experience of sitting around a table with people who are discussing the student's disability and the accommodations they may need. Parents frequently choose not to include the student in IEP meetings. They might think it may make the student uncomfortable or may be difficult for the student to hear others talk about their weaknesses. Although school districts are always required to invite students with disabilities to their IEP planning meetings, students are not required actually to attend and are often not encouraged to attend. If students do attend, they frequently do not have the self-advocacy skills to participate in the meeting. It is *crucial* in high school that students on the autism spectrum attend and participate, if possible, in all meetings concerning their needs at school.

Parents and the school can help prepare the student for such meetings by discussing with them the purpose of the meeting and who will be there. If the student is prepared for the meeting, he or she can participate more fully. The student can be given an agenda for the meeting with a time designated for the student to make a statement if appropriate. If they are going to speak, some students may need to rehearse their part ahead of time. If the student is not able to attend the meeting, or speaking to the group is too difficult, he or she can possibly write out any questions or comments they would like to see addressed. If attending the entire meeting is too much for the student, consider having him or her attend the beginning of the meeting only, long enough to hear the introductions and hear about progress the student has made. The student can also write a statement that can be read at the meeting. Any opportunity to understand the transition process and participate in self-advocating will benefit the student.

Eric's Transition Plan meeting in high school was his first experience of participating fully in a meeting about his school services. He had attended the before-school meetings with teachers to meet the teachers and introduce himself, but had not attended an IEP meeting. In retrospect, I wish I had included him earlier in other meetings so he would have had more experience in advocating for himself. I believe secondary schools should fully inform parents and students with disabilities about the emphasis on self-advocacy at the postsecondary school level. If your high school is not talking about this issue, the parent or student should be initiating discussion about this with the support team.

Other individuals attended Eric's transition meeting who did not normally attend meetings concerning him. There was a transition specialist from the school system, Eric's supervisor at his volunteer job in the community, a therapist who worked with him for years outside of school, and his grandmother. A representative from VR also attended. The Transition Plan meeting is the opportunity to invite anyone who knows and cares for the student to be involved in this important process. Parents can invite anyone they would like but should let the school know ahead of time whom they are inviting and how many people may be attending. Other family members, friends of the family, any support persons who have worked with the student, can be invited to attend. According to the law, agencies from the community that may be responsible for providing or paying for transition services to the student must be invited to the ITP meeting (Reiser 1995).

We began Eric's Transition Plan meeting with everyone introducing themselves. Each person took turns saying their name and what agency they represented or how they knew Eric. When it got to Eric's turn, his father and I were holding our breaths, not sure what Eric would say. He said, "My name is Eric, and I have autism." I was completely taken by surprise that Eric volunteered that he had autism. I knew he had been aware of his autism for years but he had never just announced it to a group of people like that. After the meeting I asked Eric why he chose to say that in particular. He said that everyone else around the table was saying their name and why they were there so he had to say something too. He knew his autism was why he was there.

The ITP meeting was very different from previous IEP meetings and not only because of the new faces around the table. This meeting was all about Eric's dreams and his goals for what he wanted to do with his life. During the meeting Eric was asked questions about what he wanted to do when he graduated from high school. They asked him about where he might want to live when he is an adult, whether he wanted to learn to drive, where he envisioned himself working. Sometimes Eric didn't have answers to the questions and would say he didn't know and that was OK. Even when he didn't have an answer it was helpful because it opened up a discussion about what options Eric might have. Eric learned more about the decisions he would eventually have to make for his future. It was a learning experience for me as his parent because Eric had not spoken about many of these things before. It was good to hear Eric's hopes and dreams for himself. When the ITP team had a better idea about Eric's goals, they discussed ways to help him reach these goals. They suggested resources within the school and the community that could possibly be helpful. They talked about the skills Eric already had and what he would need to learn. Goals were written in the Transition Plan including the names of who would be responsible for working on these goals.

The ITP meetings are a wonderful opportunity to focus on issues of self-advocacy and independent living skills needed for the student's future. In determining what needs the student may have in this area, parents, with the student, may want to consider the following questions:

- Does the student understand the disability and how it affects their learning?

- Can the student describe their strengths and weaknesses in ways others can understand?

- Does the student know what resources are available to help them?

- Does the student know how to access these resources?

- Does the student understand their legal rights in regard to accessing services?

- Does the student have the capability to live independently? If not, what skills do they need? (Heggie 1999)

The transition team can use these kinds of questions to stimulate discussion and keep the focus of the meetings on the future needs of the student.

When Eric started his junior year of high school, his sister became a freshman at the same school. It was the first time in many years that they would be attending the same school and riding the same bus to school. It was great for me as their mother to have them in the same school. The previous two years all three of my children were at different schools and life was complicated. I had concerns that socially it might be difficult for my daughter if other students asked her about her brother. Being a ninth grader entering high school can be stressful enough without adding that piece to the puzzle. As it turned out, my daughter handled it really well. There were times when new friends at school would ask her about her brother and she would explain that he had autism. She didn't bring up her autistic brother to many people as a topic of conversation but she was also not afraid to answer their questions or correct them if they made comments that were not correct.

I think parents need to be proactive and try to prevent possible difficult situations from occurring for the sibling. It is easy to forget sometimes that the sibling may be feeling accepting and proud of their brother or sister with a disability but at the same time may also be embarrassed or uncomfortable when having to explain to their peers about their differences. At the beginning of the first year Eric and my daughter were at the high school together, the bus they rode home from school was very late arriving at the high school every afternoon. The students had to wait at the school for at least a half an hour for the bus to arrive. I knew what Eric would be doing while he was waiting for the bus. He would be walking back and forth, maybe quietly talking to himself, and maybe flicking his fingers near his face. It doesn't bother people, it isn't disruptive in any way, but I knew it could cause some stares or comments from the other students. I thought that would be difficult for my daughter to have to deal with during her first weeks of high school when she was trying to adjust and find new friends. I changed my work schedule and arranged to pick them up at school each afternoon until the buses became more predictable. Parents can try to think ahead and prevent uncomfortable situations for the siblings.

An important part of preparing for college in high school is to take the standardized testing required for college entrance. In the United States, the first test students usually take is the Preliminary Scholastic Assessment Test (PSAT) or, as it is also known, the National Merit Scholarship Qualifying Test (NMSQT). The PSAT primarily serves as a practice test for students but if the student does very well on the test, it can qualify them for participation in the national merit scholarship competition. Usually the following year after taking the PSAT, the student will take one of two standardized tests. The Scholastic Assessment Test (SAT) measures the verbal and mathematical reasoning abilities of the student. The American College Testing Assessment (ACT) measures English, mathematics, reading, and science reasoning abilities. Students can choose between the two tests but many colleges will require one test or the other. Most colleges on the east coast of the United States require the SAT. Students need to research the requirement for any colleges they are considering. The student usually takes one of these tests in their junior or senior year of high school.

The scores from the SAT or ACT can be weighed heavily by colleges in choosing the students they will accept. It is a long test, four hours, and students fill in "bubbles" in an answer booklet, something that could be difficult for some students on the autism spectrum. Eric had never done particularly well on standardized testing in the past and I was not hopeful that this would be any easier. I found a computer program (Kaplan Test Prep and Admissions Courses: see Appendix A) that prepares students for how to take the PSAT, SAT, and ACT tests. The program is very interactive and entertaining, with animated characters that make jokes and guide you through practice tests and instruction on how to take the test. This was a great tool to prepare Eric. My typical kids also were helped by using this program. Students can work on the program at home for short segments of time, completing different lessons. It includes practice questions in each category. Most important, it includes strategies for how to narrow your choices of answers when you don't automatically know the correct answer. There are different computer programs that can be helpful as well as books and courses for students to help them prepare for these standardized tests. The guidance counselor at the high school should have more information about resources to prepare students for standardized testing.

Some colleges may require an applicant to take one or more SAT subject tests in certain areas of study. The SAT II tests, as they are called, are offered in English, mathematics, many sciences, history, and foreign languages. They measure the extent of a student's knowledge about a particular subject. Often the best time to take these tests is immediately following completion of a course on that subject. Students should check whether a college they want to attend requires any of these tests.

If a student is enrolled in advanced placement (AP) courses, they will also take a standardized test at the completion of these courses. AP courses are college-level courses that prepare the student for college-level work while still in high school. If the student makes a score of three or higher on a scale of one to five, they can usually receive advanced placement in a college course or credit for having taken a college course. Be aware that the student in an AP class must take the AP exam at the end of the course unless they get written permission from the administration at the school not to take the test. At the time of writing this, the cost of taking an AP exam is around $85. This is less than the cost of taking the course at college but if the student doesn't make a score of three or higher, it may be a loss of that money. Also, not all colleges will give credit for AP courses, or will require a higher score than a three on the AP test. The student should check the policy of each college they are considering.

All the tests described above are part of the College Board standardized testing program. Accommodations on all College Board tests are available for students with disabilities who are eligible. The Services for Students with Disabilities (SSD) department within the College Board determines whether a student qualifies for accommodations. A student must submit an SSD Student Eligibility Form requesting accommodations. These forms can be found and submitted through the guidance counselor at the high school. The parent, student, and guidance counselor complete and sign the form. Accommodations offered that might be helpful to students on the autism spectrum include extended time, larger type and non-bubble answer sheet, cassette/reader, writer/scribe, use of computer for the writing or essay part of the test, and extra or extended breaks (College Board 2005).

To be eligible for accommodations on the College Board tests the following criteria must be met:

- The student must have a disability that requires accommodations.

- There must be documentation that supports the need for testing accommodations.

- The student must also be receiving the accommodations, due to the disability, on school-based tests.

Therefore, if the student thinks they will need accommodations on any of the College Board tests in high school, they should also have testing accommodations included in the student's IEP. It would be advantageous for the student and parents to review the "Instructions for Completing the Student Eligibility Form for Accomodations on College Board Tests Based on Disability" from the College Board (see Appendix A) as early as the eighth grade when preparing the IEP for the transition to high school. Then if the student is already receiving extended time on tests or other testing accommodations in the IEP, they should qualify for this same accommodation on the standardized college tests. When scheduling any of the College Board tests, there may be limited dates available where extended time or other accommodations are permitted. It is not advisable to wait too late to pursue this through the high school guidance office.

Once an Eligibility Form is sent and approved, a student does not need to reapply for accommodations on future College Board tests unless he or she changes high schools. Also, if a student wants to take a future test without accommodations they can. They would only need to send in the test registration without the Eligibility Form. If a student takes a College Board test with accommodations due to a disability, the student's scores that are sent to prospective colleges will not show that accommodations were given. There are really no reasons why a student shouldn't use accommodations if they are needed and the student qualifies. Eric took the PSAT and SAT with a smaller group of students in the library with extended time. He scored better than we expected and I think having the accommodations helped him.

In addition to test scores, colleges will pay close attention to any extra-curricular activities the student has participated in during high school. Clubs, sports, and volunteering in the community or at the school are some of the activities normally listed on college applications. For the student on the autism spectrum, this may be a weak area. The student may feel uncomfortable joining clubs or may not have the physical skills to participate in sports. Volunteering in the community or at the high school may be a better way to get extra-curricular activities for college applications. The colleges are looking for *sustained* participation in an activity that broadens a student's experiences and makes him or her a better-rounded student. There may be a cause or a program in the community that interests the student and where they can volunteer their time.

For some high school students on the autism spectrum who wonder if college is a realistic option, it may be helpful to explore summer pre-college courses. During the summer after their junior or senior year the student can enroll in a college course at a college in the area. There are particular colleges in the United States that offer pre-college programs specifically to help students make the transition to college successfully. The MAAP Services for Autism and Asperger Syndrome, Inc. has compiled a list of some of these transition programs. You can find their website listed in Appendix A.

The Tech Prep Program is another option for students with disabilities to help prepare them for careers requiring education or training beyond high school. It involves a course of study that helps high school students learn more technical facts and skills. This program is a result of the Carl D. Perkins Act of 1990. It consists of two years of high school and two years of postsecondary education designed to lead to an associate degree in a specific field. The curriculum focuses on the areas of mathematics, science, communications, and technologies (NICHCY 1991). You and your child will need to check with your school to see if such a program is available in your area.

Students on the autism spectrum in high school also need to seriously consider how they will be able to handle the stress of college. No matter how many accommodations that are arranged, no matter how much support students receive, they will most likely experience stress at college. The stress may come from many sources—academic, social, health, decision-making, etc. Preparing the high school student for the expectation of stressful situations is very important. A plan for the student can be developed and practiced while still in high school. Goals to work on stress reduction or preventing stress can be included in the IEP. The student may need certain strategies to follow when feeling overwhelmed that are individualized to the student. A quiet place a student can go to be alone may need to be designated. A regular exercise routine can help prevent the build-up of stress. The student may have activities that are calming for them that can be done when they are anxious such as listening to music, reading books, or having particular objects to handle or hold. Developing a plan in high school to combat stress, practicing it and helping the student know when they need it, can be crucial for a student to survive the stress of college.

In college the student on the autism spectrum will frequently be challenged by understanding the perspectives of others. Attending college requires a great deal of perspective taking. The student must understand the perspective of the instructor so they can meet the expectations of an assignment or know how to answer an essay question on an exam. The student may not agree with the instructor's perspective but they have to tolerate it. The college student will frequently be asked in English classes to describe the perspective of a writer or the perspective of the protagonist in a story. The student must also understand the different perspectives of the other students living in the dormitory. Not everyone will make the same choices in college and the student may have difficulty understanding the choices of others. All of these situations can be complicated for the student on the autism spectrum. Parents and teachers in high school and earlier, if possible, should look for teachable opportunities related to perspective taking. Find and explain situations where the student has a different perspective than another person. The student may not always understand the perspective of another, but they can become accustomed to differing points of view and how to react to them.

By the end of high school the student will, one hopes, know what they want to do and will have made a decision about what comes next in their life. The following chapter describes the process of deciding whether college is the right choice and, if so, how to choose between the many options available to students.

3 Making the Decision about College

There are many differences between college and high school that should be considered very carefully by students on the autism spectrum and their parents when making the decision whether college is the right option. There are important differences in the laws that protect students with disabilities in college. The responsibilities of the student, the instructors, and the parents are different in college than in high school. The academics will most likely be harder than anything the student has experienced before. The level of independence required in college can be a challenge for many students on the autism spectrum. Parents and the student should discuss the many differences between college and high school as the first step in preparing the student for the transition.

Unless the student attends a private high school, their education up to this point has been mandatory and free. Going to college is completely voluntary and the tuition and expenses to attend can be very expensive, especially if the student chooses a private college. Not everyone who desires to go to college will necessarily be admitted. Students with disabilities cannot be discriminated against for admission purposes but they must meet the admission criteria for the college they want to attend. The student must also continue to meet the academic standards set by the college to remain a student there.

A student who struggles in the public school setting is protected because the school is required to serve that student. College does not have to serve a student who is failing or having trouble adjusting. For a student in college who has a documented disability and needs accommodations to help with academics, the school is required to make "reasonable" accommodations. In the college setting students are ensured "access" to programs and services. This does not necessarily mean that changes will be made to the programs or courses so that the student can succeed. The college can provide an academic accommodation only if that accommodation does not change the outcome of the course or the requirements of the program. Most important, the college will not automatically put accommodations in place. The student has to pursue accommodations if they are needed.

Classes are typically very different in college compared to high school. A student in high school is accustomed to following a strict schedule of school-mandated classes, going from one class to another during the day. In college students must manage their own time and make their own schedules. In high school the student spends approximately 6 hours a day or 30 hours a week in class. In college, a student will usually spend between 12 and 17 hours in classes each week. There may be long periods of time between classes when students must decide how to spend their time and their decisions on the use of this time can be critical to their chances for success. Depending on the size of the college, classes are often much larger than in high school, with sometimes over one hundred students in a class. Attendance is mandatory in high school and well monitored, but in college attendance policies can vary by instructor. Students must be responsible for making their own decisions about attending classes in college. Textbooks for classes in high school are free but in college the average cost of books per semester for a full-time student can range between $250 and $500. In high school, the student has guidance from counselors and parents to know what classes to take to be able to graduate. In college the graduation requirements are more complicated and the student must know the graduation requirements for their particular course of study or have someone to guide them carefully in their course selections.

The instructors of college classes have different responsibilities and roles than the teachers of high school classes. In high school, teachers often grade and check homework, remind students of upcoming projects and tests, and remind students of missed assignments. They also typically provide students with missed information following an absence. In college, the instructor often assumes homework is complete and may not check it at all. When a student misses a class in college the instructor expects the student to get information they missed from other students. In college it is not unusual to have an instructor, a graduate student possibly, who has not taught before and has not been formally trained in teaching. Teachers in high school usually present information to help the student understand the material in the textbook. An instructor in college may lecture during the entire class time and may not follow the textbook at all. The student in college must be able to connect the textbook with the lectures when they study for tests. In high school the teachers will approach a student if they believe they need help. In college the instructors are usually open and helpful but they expect the student to initiate contact if assistance is needed.

Studying requirements in college are also quite different than in high school. It is generally recommended that a college student study at least two to three hours outside of class for each hour spent in class. For a 15-hour course load (a typical course load for a student in college) students would need to study 30–45 hours a week in addition to the time they spend in classes. Studying in college also involves a substantial amount of reading outside of class which may not be directly addressed in class. Because of the fast pace of the coursework, the student must review lecture notes and material in the textbook regularly to stay caught up in a class. In college it is also important that students be able to successfully use the library and its resources. Most college students will need to spend a great deal of time in the library doing research for their courses.

The amount of testing a college student receives can be very different from that of a high school student. In high school the teachers typically give frequent tests covering small amounts of material. Teachers often give students review sheets or a written list of what may be covered on a test. High school teachers usually allow make-up tests and provide review sessions in class before tests. In college there may be only two to three tests during a semester and the tests may cover large amounts of material. Students are expected to organize their material to prepare for tests. Some instructors will not have tests at all but will require papers or projects instead. Make-up tests are seldom offered in college and have to be requested by the student. College instructors may not offer review sessions, and may instead expect the student to find study groups. In high school, grades on tests and papers weigh heavily towards the final grade in a class. However, there are often homework and extra credit grades that can raise the cumulative grade if the test scores are low. In college, tests and major papers may provide the entire grade for the course. Extra credit work is not normally used to raise a grade. In high school, students show they have learned the material by reproducing what they were taught or by solving the kinds of problems they were shown how to solve. In college, the student's knowledge of the material is more often judged by their ability to apply what they have learned to new situations or to solve new problems.

Grades are given for most assigned work in high school but in college grades may not be given for some assignments. In high school a student can graduate as long as they have passed all required courses with a grade D or higher. Most college programs require a student to have a minimum of a 2.0 grade point average to graduate. (2.0 translates to a grade C average.) The work required to obtain an A or B in college will be harder. There are no "weighted" courses in college where students can get grade points to add to their final grade because of the difficulty of the course. In college, students may be put on academic probation if their grade point average for a semester is low. They will usually then be given a set period of time to bring up their grades or they can be suspended from school.

Behavior problems are normally not tolerated at college. Not only do the college students have to be responsible for their behavior in class, they are also responsible for their behavior outside of class—in the dormitory, at sporting events, or in any other activities on campus. Because college students are considered adults, they are treated as adults and expected to behave appropriately. In high school, behavioral problems are much more the norm due to the relative immaturity of the student population, and this may serve to make problematic behaviors of a student on the autism spectrum seem less severe.

Once the student and family considers the differences between college and high school, they must focus on what is right for the individual student. Does the student like going to school? Will going to college be overly stressful for the student? What does the student want to do in the future and does it require a college degree? They must also consider the non-academic aspects of college such as the social, self-help and independence skills that students will need.

Having worked in the field of autism for many years, I have been fortunate to meet a number of adults on the spectrum who have attended college. Many do well and enjoy attending college but upon graduation have major difficulties finding jobs and keeping them. The social component of the workplace can be stressful for individuals on the autism spectrum. Although the student may have been able to learn the material required for a particular degree, that doesn't necessarily mean that they have the work skills an individual in that field needs. A degree from college will not guarantee competitive employment following graduation. Parents need to keep this in mind when thinking about college as an option for the student on the autism spectrum.

In order to make our own decision about college as an option for our son, my husband and I asked ourselves some questions. Would Eric be able to handle the independence required in college? Would he be able to set an alarm to wake up, pick out the right clothes, find something to eat, and get to class on time? Would he be safe at college? We knew he was more vulnerable than most students and wondered if he would be able to make smart and safe decisions. We also asked ourselves how it would affect Eric if he failed. We knew the academics at the college level would be harder than anything he had done before. If he didn't do well and failed, how would that affect his self-esteem? Up to this point Eric was feeling very good about himself, and we didn't want that to change. Keeping all this in mind and considering the expense, the hard work, the possible stress and anxiety, we had to decide if his going to college would be worth it.

After a great deal of thought and discussion, Eric's father and I decided that despite our concerns, we wanted Eric to have the experience of college just as we wanted it for our other two children. We didn't want to close any doors just because we didn't think Eric could do it or because we were scared for him. He had surprised us numerous times over the years when we misjudged his abilities. Eric might do well in college and we wanted him to have the opportunity to try.

To be able to talk more with Eric about choices for his future, I needed to educate myself about the different college choices that might be available to him. I began researching college options in our area and was pleased to discover that there were several different ones available to us. Eric could live at home and attend a local community college, live at home and commute to a nearby four-year college, or live on campus at a college somewhere in our state. We ruled out any colleges outside of our state because of the cost for out-of-state tuition and because we felt there were many good colleges within our state that could meet Eric's needs.

As we entered Eric's senior year of high school it was time to make a definite decision and to find out exactly what Eric wanted to do. This was not as easy as it sounds. Eric didn't know whether he wanted to continue in school after graduating from high school or go to work full time. He didn't understand what the college experience would be like. Most high school students talk about college with each other. They may know students who have gone to college or they follow sports at local colleges. They may watch movies or television shows that take place in a college setting. Eric did none of these things and was somewhat clueless as to what going to college meant. I knew he had never particularly enjoyed school over the years and always lived for his summer break. But I also knew that the school environment would be very different at college and he might very well like the independence and flexibility of a college student's schedule.

The first step to help Eric understand more about college and be able to make his own decision was to take him to some college campuses near our home. We visited a technical school in our town and two large state universities nearby. We walked around the campuses looking at dormitories and classrooms. We made sure we visited the campuses when school was in session so that he would get to see students walking to classes, sitting together outside, or studying in the library. My husband and I also talked with him about our own college experiences—what was fun, what was difficult, and how it was different from being in high school.

In order to make a decision about college, Eric also needed to understand what it would be like to work instead of going to school. To give him work experience, Eric had been volunteering in different jobs since middle school. He had paid jobs during two summers in high school. Because of his special interest in animals, Eric's volunteer and paid jobs all involved working around animals. He worked in an animal shelter cleaning cat cages and feeding the animals. He also worked in the animal department at a local museum where he maintained the animal exhibit areas and helped with some small-animal care. He worked one summer at a wild bird rescue center doing various jobs. These were valuable work experiences for him as he learned the importance of being punctual, following directions, and getting along with others.

Working or volunteering during the years before graduating from high school can also help students learn more about their particular interests. Exploring different work settings can give the student ideas about what they may or may not want to do for a living. Working in certain jobs may show the student exactly what they don't want to do or what they don't have the skills to do. Having successful job experiences might help the student find a future career path or decide on an area to study in college. Although many students on the autism spectrum have intense interests or skills that can be pursued for a career, not all students will have interests that can translate into a future career. Volunteer or paid work experience before going to college may help them find new areas they may be interested in pursuing.

When it was time for Eric to decide his plans for after graduation, we discussed his work experiences. We talked about what he liked about his jobs and what he didn't like. I shared some of my own experiences with jobs and what was positive and negative to me about working full-time. We also talked about the money he would receive for working and the importance of having money for things he enjoys as well as for living expenses such as rent, utilities, and food.

After visiting the schools and talking about the experience of working full-time, Eric and I talked about the positives and negatives of both options. It may also be helpful for some students to make a written list of the pros and cons of both options so they can visually see the differences. Whether written down or discussed, the process of weighing the pros and cons for different choices helps students learn a strategy for making decisions, something they will need to do independently throughout their lives. When we finished our discussion of the positives and negatives of college and work, it was clear to Eric and to me that he wanted to give college a try.

The next step is to decide where to apply to college. There are many factors to consider when choosing a college. These factors are relevant for all students deciding on a college but may be especially important for the student on the autism spectrum. The student needs to consider the curriculum offered by the school, the size and location of the school, and the supports that are available there. Each of these factors should be weighed in relation to the individual needs and interests of the student.

It is important that the college offers a curriculum that appeals to the student. The student may not yet know what they want to major in, but they probably have certain interests or subjects where they excel. The student should explore whether or not a college offers courses in their area of interest. Some larger universities may want incoming freshmen to declare a major or choose a particular college or department within the university before entering. At the university Eric attends, freshmen enter a college within the university such as the College of Humanities and Social Sciences, the College of Engineering, the College of Education, etc. Each college offers multiple majors and degrees within that field. Depending on the number of students each college can accept, the student may face significant competition for admission. For example, a student who states on their admissions application that they want to enter the College of Engineering will have to compete against other future engineers applying to the university.

There are advantages to this model. The student can enter a college within a university that offers courses of special interest to the student. These courses may be easier and less anxiety-provoking for the beginning student. The student will still have to take the required general education courses that may be less interesting and more difficult, but they can combine them with the less stressful courses in their major. Another advantage of this model is that the student is assigned an academic advisor within the department. That academic advisor is usually a professor in the department, someone who has experience in the field and knows about careers in that area of interest. Most of the colleges within the university also offer an orientation class for students within that college. Freshmen learn introductory information about educational requirements, resources that are available, and careers related to that particular field. Starting in a particular major during the first year of college also gives the student the time to evaluate whether their chosen field of study is what they really want to do. The downside to this is that if the student realizes they have chosen the wrong major they may have to formally change colleges within the university. This can delay the projected time for graduation.

At Eric's university, those students who aren't sure what they want to major in enter what is called "First Year College." Students are required to take a wide variety of courses to expose them to many different areas of study. Students in First Year College are also housed together with other students who are undecided in what they want to study. These students are given opportunities to meet with representatives of the different colleges on campus. They are given an interests survey to help them discover where their interests lie and what their skills are. They are also encouraged to participate in cultural, academic, and social events on campus. This could be a good option for those students who don't have a specific area of interest and those students who would benefit from a more social "group" environment. For some students on the autism spectrum this would be difficult. Parents and students need to explore the options each individual university or college offers for incoming freshmen.

Eric's university also has an "institute" within the college that focuses on agriculture studies. Students enroll in two-year programs within the institute which lead to an Associate degree. Students take courses on the same campus as students in the four-year programs, are taught by the same faculty, and can live on campus. However, the students do not have the same requirements to enroll. It can be a good option for students who want a focused curriculum and training for a career but do not have the competitive test scores or grades to enroll in the four-year program. Students also have the option to transfer into the four-year program at a later time if their grades are acceptable, which might be a good transition program for some students who need more time to adjust to the academics of college. Parents and the student should explore whether programs such as this exist at the colleges being considered.

Another factor to consider when choosing a college or university is the size of the school. This can be especially important if the student does not do well in large crowds. In my son's school of 30,000-plus students, there are always crowds in the dining halls, the bookstore, walking to and from classes, wherever Eric goes on campus. If that would be a problem for the student, a smaller school may be more appropriate. Smaller colleges will have smaller classes and more opportunities to get individual attention from instructors if needed. They also will have less challenging campuses to navigate and perhaps more opportunities to connect with other students socially. The bureaucracy may be easier to deal with at the smaller schools. Larger colleges or universities, however, can give the student more anonymity and some students on the autism spectrum may prefer this. Eric likes the large classes with over a hundred students because he doesn't usually have to participate in class or be called upon directly. Large colleges or universities also offer more choices of courses, campus activities, and clubs. If the student wants to broaden their horizon in an area of study, there will usually be more options to choose from at a larger university. The size of the school should be chosen based on what the student will be able to tolerate and what the student's individual needs might be.

If the student is going to college from a home schooling situation or from a small private secondary school, the size of the college may be especially important. The students may be used to individualized attention or very small class sizes. Smaller colleges may demand less of an adjustment from the student. Parents of students coming from home schools or private schools also need to ask about the testing requirements or documentation requirements needed for each college that is being considered. If the student has not had previous IEPs or school evaluations, the college may require specific kinds of documentation to qualify the student for supports from the disabilities services office.

The location of the college or university is also very important. If the student will be commuting, the school needs to be located within a convenient distance. If the student doesn't drive, consider finding a college that is conveniently reachable by public transport. Parents also need to consider how close to home the student should be if they are going to need their parents' support while in college. Students on the autism spectrum often have high test scores and grades and can meet admission criteria for prestigious universities that may be located far away from home. As much as this may be attractive to the student and the family, they should also consider the competitiveness and the difficulty of the academics at these universities as well as the distance the student may be from the supports at home.

Some students on the autism spectrum can successfully attend college long distances from home. A friend's son, who attends a smaller, prestigious school several states away, is doing well there. The student and his parents chose that particular college because the student needed a smaller school setting and the mother had attended the school and knew it was an accepting and responsive environment. There would also be a few family members nearby who could be supports for the student if needed. This student had spent a fair amount of time away from home during summers at camps and traveling and had done well with those experiences. This particular student possessed the skills needed for this level of independence and going to college fairly far away from home has been a good choice.

In addition to the curriculum, size, and location of a college or university, students and parents should consider the strength of the Disabilities Services program there. This support program may be called different names depending on the school or the country where the school is located, but the services are often very similar. It is beneficial if the disabilities support office of the school has had experience with students on the autism spectrum, but is not absolutely necessary. It is equally as important that the school is willing to learn about the disability and to consider the needs of each student individually. In addition to exploring what accommodations in academics are available, you may also want to ask about tutoring and counseling services on campus. These supports should be available as well. Most students on the autism spectrum can also benefit from personal and organizational support services such as a personal "coach." Although these supports are rarely offered through Disabilities Services on campus, it is important to ask about them. Some colleges may have creative ways to offer these supports through other offices within the college or through individuals or agencies in the community.

During Eric's senior year of high school we met with a service provider from the Disabilities Services office at a nearby university that Eric was considering. He had already applied to that university but had not yet been accepted. We met with her to learn about resources that would be available for him there. We also wanted to make sure that Eric would meet the requirements and have the necessary documentation to receive services. The meeting was very helpful and I highly recommend that parents and students visit the Disabilities Services office of every school that is being considered.

When meeting with a member of the Disabilities Services program, the student and parents should get as much information as possible about the program and its support to students on the autism spectrum. You may want to consider asking some of the following questions:

- What kinds of supports are available for students on the autism spectrum?

- What documentation is required for accessing services for this disability?

- What possible academic accommodations would a student on the autism spectrum qualify for?

- Does your program have experience working with students on the autism spectrum?

- Do members of the Disabilities Services staff receive any special training in autism spectrum disorders?

- Is the staff within the Disabilities Services office full-time or part-time?

- What is a typical case load for a service provider in your program?

- How often can a student meet with a service provider?

- What can Disabilities Services do to help a student during the course selection and registration process?

- What role does Disabilities Services play during the freshman orientation process?

- How does a student access tutoring help at this college?

- Who does the tutoring, staff or students?

- How does a student access personal counseling help?

- Does the program offer help for the student with self-advocacy skills (i.e. accompanying the student to a meeting with an instructor, role playing or other preparations for advocating)?

- How do faculty members at this college accept students with disabilities?

- Does the program offer training or education to the faculty members working with students with certain disabilities?

- Are there any support groups or social opportunities specifically available for students with this disability?

- What supports are available for students on the autism spectrum in the area of career counseling?

- Are there internships available for students with disabilities?

- Who can parents contact if they have concerns during the school year?

Your questions may be different than these and should be based on the specific needs of the student. Whatever your questions or concerns, it is very important that the student be involved in this meeting and have the opportunity to ask any questions that will help them learn more about the college and its supports. How the office reacts to the student and to the parents, how welcoming they are to the student, and how open they are to questions can give you good information towards making a decision about that college.

The first meeting Eric and I had with Disabilities Services opened my eyes to how important it was for Eric to be able to advocate for himself. During our meeting with the service provider, I was surprised by how she was not directing any questions to me but was speaking directly to Eric. She would ask him a question about whether or not he thought he would need a certain accommodation in class. Eric would look a little bewildered and look over at me and say, "I don't know, Mom, will I?" I knew then that I should have gotten Eric more involved in his IEP process in high school and should have talked to him more about the areas where he often needs help. The skill of self-advocacy may be the most important skill the student with a disability will need in college.

In addition to considering the size, location, curriculum, and supports of possible colleges, the student and the parents should also compare the various kinds of schools that are available. In the United States there are many options a student can choose from in addition to the popular four-year college or university. There are community colleges and technical schools, two-year colleges or junior colleges, and more specialized schools such as business or nursing schools. There are also some colleges that specialize in serving the needs of students with learning disabilities such as autism or Asperger Syndrome. The student should explore all the different options that may be available to see which kinds of colleges would meet their needs.

Community colleges provide a good option for many students on the autism spectrum. The requirements to get into a community college may be less rigorous than those for a larger state university or college. Community colleges usually have an open enrollment policy which means they accept students with a high school diploma or who have taken the General Education Development test (GED). Standardized College Board tests are generally not required. The cost of a community college is usually well below that of a four-year public or private college. Financial aid resources may also be more readily available at a community college. The "community" in community colleges is an important part of the mission of these colleges. The student body reflects the population of the community where the school is located, and businesses and agencies within the community are typically involved in the college.

Some community colleges offer courses for students who are still in high school. The student on the autism spectrum can take a course during the last year of high school or during the summer before graduation and gain some good experience to prepare them for college. Then if they choose to attend that particular community college following graduation, the transition may be easier.

Classes are usually smaller at a community college and may average from 20 to 40 students. As mentioned before, classes at a larger four-year university can easily have over a hundred students. Smaller classes may be helpful for those students who learn better in smaller groups or in quieter settings. If the student gets overwhelmed in crowds, community colleges may be a good choice. Due to the smaller class size, at a community college the student may have the opportunity to get to know the instructors better. Academic accommodations are also available in community colleges and the disabilities support services can be very good.

Many community colleges or technical schools have programs in which students can take the general college-required classes there, and then can transfer into a four-year college later. This might give the student the extra time they need to learn the skills necessary to be successful in a larger college setting. However, transferring at a later date into a four-year college requires another transition for the student. For students who don't like change, this may be difficult. Before choosing this option, the parents and student should look carefully at whether the community college courses they will be taking will transfer to the university.

A technical or trade school is usually a two-year institution that offers occupational programs to help prepare students for employment. They primarily offer courses related to engineering and physical sciences but will typically offer courses related to the liberal arts as well. Technical schools can be a good option for students on the autism spectrum because they can concentrate on their particular interest if it is one offered by the school. My own experience with a local technical school is that they had good supports for students with disabilities but they did not offer the kinds of courses that my son was interested in studying.

Another option to consider when looking at the kinds of schools available is the two-year college or junior college. Whereas community colleges usually serve students living in a particular community, junior colleges often enroll students from outside their geographical area. The tuition at a junior college may be higher than tuition at a community college. Junior colleges also typically have residence halls for students and community colleges generally do not.

Two-year colleges may offer more academic support than is offered at four-year colleges. Classes are typically smaller and are taught by faculty, not teaching assistants. A junior college or a two-year program may be good for the student who has difficulty planning very far ahead. The student can work towards an Associate degree first, and then plan what to do next. A large percentage of students continue on to four-year colleges following their junior college experience. This could be another option for the student who needs some time to develop self-confidence and academic and social skills before attempting a four-year program. If a student is considering a particular junior college they should ask the school what kind of grades they would need in order to transfer, and into which four-year colleges most students from that junior college transfer.

A business school is another type of institution that may be an option for a student on the autism spectrum. Some business schools offer predominantly business or secretarial courses. Others may offer a more extensive program including liberal arts courses in addition to business courses. Most programs will offer a two-year Associate degree.

Another issue that must be addressed by the student and the parents is whether the student will disclose their disability when applying to a college or university. This will depend on many factors and will ultimately be the decision of the student. There may be no reason to disclose at this stage of the process if the student's academic scores and course selections in high school qualify them for admission into the chosen school. However, if there are circumstances that need to be explained about the student's academic history or any weaknesses that are noticeable on the application, some explanation may be necessary. More information on the issue of self-disclosure is included in Chapter 7.

Disclosure about a diagnosis may be necessary for application to some schools. There is a limited number of colleges that are specifically modeled to meet the needs of students on the autism spectrum or students with learning disabilities. The College Internship Program, with its two locations at the Brevard Center in Melbourne, Florida, and at the Berkshire Center in Lee, Massachusetts, is one such program. According to the College Internship Program websites for the two centers, they provide individualized academic, internship and independent living experiences for students with Asperger Syndrome and nonverbal learning differences. Students live in apartments with other students and receive support and instruction in money management, cooking skills, and cleaning and apartment maintenance. They are also offered social and recreational support. Academically, the student receives support from an academic coordinator and from tutors. Students can participate in individual and small group instruction and receive assistance in time management and organizational skills. Some students attend classes at local colleges in the area where they can receive accommodations. Counseling is also available to students on an individual basis or in group sessions. The Brevard and Berkshire Centers also offer individual training modules designed specifically for students with Asperger Syndrome or nonverbal learning differences. These modules may include social stories, instruction in disclosure, theory of mind, sensory integration, coaching and role play, and biomedical interventions. Tuition ranges from $33,000 per year to $58,000 per year. Room and board are approximately $1000 per month (College Internship Program—Berkshire Center 2004; College Internship Program—Brevard Center 2004.)

Minnesota Life College is another program serving students with learning disabilities including Asperger Syndrome and high-functioning autism. The program stresses independent living skills, social skills development, and decision-making. Students also receive help in the area of health and wellness through fitness programs and recreational activities. Students live in apartments while they work, do internships, or attend traditional postsecondary schools.

In addition to having a learning disability or related neurological condition, incoming students at Minnesota Life College are required to be at least 18 years of age, have completed K-12 education and have a score of 70 or above on intellectual testing. Students must also have the ability to volunteer or work with minimal supervision and have stable behavior and impulse control. This is a three-year program and costs approximately $28,000 a year for tuition and room and board (Minnesota Life College 2003).

The College Program for Students with Higher Functioning Autism at Marshall University in Huntington, West Virginia, is another program specifically for students on the autism spectrum. Developed by the West Virginia Autism Training Center, the program provides academic, social, and life skills support to Marshall University students with high-functioning autism or Asperger Syndrome. The overall goal of the program is to develop strategies based on the student's individual needs that will assist the student to successfully earn a college degree. Faculty, tutors, and students at the university are given training related to autism and the unique learning style of students on the autism spectrum. Each student, with their family's help, participates in person-centered planning activities and develops the student's individual support plan. When the student begins classes an assistant may be assigned to help them in transitioning from class to class. Students check in regularly with staff to discuss any concerns or issues. The College Program for Students with Higher Functioning Autism is a small program, designed to serve only ten students, but it offers a model for other colleges and universities. Students on the autism spectrum in this program pay the same tuition fees paid by the other students at Marshall University (West Virginia Autism Training Center 2004).

Whatever kind of college or university is selected, parents and the student should also seriously consider the amount of participation in college that the student can handle. Some students may need to work their way gradually to a full-time school schedule. A student could live at home and take one or two classes at the college to familiarize themselves with the environment. Then they could add more classes as they show they can handle the academic responsibilities. Commuting may be a good option if the student needs some time to adjust to going to college before moving away from home. Colleges frequently have "commuter lounges." These are areas where students who commute can study or meet and socialize between classes. For some students, working part-time and attending college part-time is a good option. If the student has difficulty with the college environment, it is also possible to take online or video courses at some colleges. Parents and students need to explore what is available in their community and then carefully evaluate which college situation would best meet their needs.

The cost of the tuition and expenses for a college may be an important factor in a family's choice. Private colleges or universities may offer smaller class size and more individual attention from instructors, but may be too expensive for some families to afford without some sort of financial aid. Financial aid is available for students from a number of sources. Anyone who feels they don't have the resources to cover all of the college expenses should apply for financial aid. The types of aid available include grants, loans, work-study, and scholarships. Loans, money borrowed to help pay college costs, are typically the only kind of financial aid that needs to be paid back. Work-study is employment that lets a student earn money toward school costs while enrolled in college. The high school guidance counselor or the financial aid office of the college or university will be able to help the student and family research what options are available.

Gifts or awards of money called scholarships are also available for students, with or without disabilities, to help with the costs of college. Scholarships are fairly competitive for students and a high grade point average or high test scores are often needed to qualify. Once awarded a scholarship, the student must retain a certain minimum grade point average while in college or risk losing their scholarship. This could place added pressure on the student with autism.

There are unique situations that can make a student eligible for certain scholarships. These might include the ethnic background or religious affiliation of the student. The parents' place or type of work can sometimes qualify a student for a particular scholarship. Sometimes the student's career goals or extra-curricular activities can qualify them for certain scholarships. The guidance counselor at the high school should have more information on how to pursue private scholarships.

There are very few scholarships available that are based on disability. Frequently the amount of money that may be available is not substantial and is generally $500 to $1000 per year. The George Washington University HEATH Resource Center has developed a listing of organizations that provide scholarships for people with particular disabilities. Their website is listed in Appendix A (HEATH Resource Center 2003).

In the United States many students with disabilities receive financial assistance from state Vocational Rehabilitation (VR) agencies. To be eligible for services, an individual must "have an impairment that results in a substantial impediment to employment and can benefit from and requires VR services for employment" (HEATH Resource Center 2003, p.7). College is considered training for employment, and if students on the autism spectrum have been determined eligible, they may receive financial assistance with college expenses. Depending on the needs of the student, VR may be able to help pay for tuition expenses, room and board, transportation expenses, and books and supplies.

VR has been a resource for my family in helping with college expenses. The first year of college, the financial assistance we received from VR was based on Eric's disability only, not on financial need. By Eric's second year of college there were budget cuts and funding restrictions and the eligibility for services was changed to include financial need as well as the student's disability. Many students living at home with their parents may not qualify for financial need because determination of need is based on the income level of the parents. However, if students receive Social Security Income (SSI), they automatically qualify for VR financial assistance.

Eric applied for SSI when he turned 18. For adults who are past their eighteenth birthday, financial need for SSI is based on the income level of the adult with the disability, not the income level of their family. A student going to college often has little income and can easily meet the financial qualifications. The student cannot have substantial amounts of money in their name. If they are considering SSI as a future option, parents of younger children with a disability need to know that having money or savings in the name of the individual with the disability may disqualify them from receiving SSI in the future. The severity of the disability is also important for qualifying for SSI. Although there is a great deal of paperwork involved and the process is fairly lengthy, the student and the parents should explore this option. More information can be found on VR and SSI by going to the DisabilityInfo.gov website listed in Appendix A.

After considering all the factors about colleges that would be important for Eric, he applied to two universities near our home. One was a university in our city and the other was a larger university in a city close to where we live. We were also considering the technical community college nearby. I envisioned Eric going to the community college and living at home and later transferring to a four-year college. But Eric really wanted to live on a college campus and the community college was not residential.

We were happy when Eric was accepted at both universities. In deciding between the two schools, we looked closely at the disabilities services and the courses offered by each university. The university farther from our home offered degrees in animal-related fields which were of interest to Eric. We also knew the university farther from home had worked with students on the autism spectrum before. Eric weighed both options and decided there were more advantages to the larger state university. We sent the necessary paperwork and money and Eric was officially enrolled in college.

It was a relief to have the final decision made and to focus on the next steps of the process. There was planning and a great deal of preparation to do. I wanted to support my son through this transition as best I could. I also wanted to be available to help him if he needed me at college, but I was not sure what my role would be. If you are a parent of a son or daughter on the autism spectrum you may have been, like me, the primary advocate for your child during their earlier school years. Parents are frequently the ones who make the calls, attend the meetings, help with homework, and fight the battles for their kids. With children as unique and challenging as ours are, we must often face years of educating others about the autism spectrum and explaining the uniqueness of our kids.

However, once your child is over 18 and is entering college, the role of the parent suddenly changes. Legally the college or university cannot share information with the parents about the student, unless they get permission from the student. Grades are not sent to parents unless the student requests it in writing. The school's purpose is to meet the needs of the student, not the needs of the parents, and they expect the students to report their own needs and initiate any requests for services or help. They cannot answer parents' questions about how the student is doing, and they won't necessarily follow parents' suggestions for ways to help the student. This is a huge change for parents who have been highly involved in advocating for their children in the past.

Parents may not be as involved in many of the day-to-day issues facing the student in college, but they can still be a significant support to the student. One way that parents can be supportive to their child in college is by helping prepare them for the changes that are coming. In the next chapter, ways parents can help students through this important transition are discussed.

4 Everything You Need to Know about Life: A Summer of Lessons

It was official. Eric had been accepted into college and was going to live in the dormitory. I was very happy and so proud of him. Then the reality of it all started to sink in. I suddenly realized that I had approximately three months to teach Eric everything he needed to know about life. I know that sounds ridiculous and was obviously impossible. Eric was going to leave home and be on his own for the first time and needed to know how to take care of himself. I kept thinking of all the things he hadn't done before and all the things he didn't know. How could I possibly teach him what he needed to know in such a short period of time?

Eric and I could spend the entire summer talking and still not cover everything that might help him adjust to college. Knowing how much Eric dislikes long spontaneous conversations, I needed to find a better way to help him prepare for the changes he would be facing. I decided to have scheduled meetings or "lessons" with Eric. We wrote them on a calendar so Eric would know when to expect them. I also informed him ahead of time what we would be discussing so he could be prepared. Sometimes I gave him information to read ahead of a meeting so he could develop questions he might have on that topic. We met approximately once a week throughout the summer. The discussions were not only about academics, but also about things he needed to know to take care of himself and be safe.

This strategy of the parent and student taking the time to talk about the upcoming transition to college can be useful for any family going through this experience. Parents may decide to have scheduled meetings as I did or impromptu discussions whenever they think of something important or whenever the student asks a question. The student's receptiveness is the key. They must want to participate and be given the opportunity to speak about any concerns they may have. Developing good communication between the parents and the student is an important first step to building a support system for the student in college.

The topics to discuss will vary and should be based on the parents' primary concerns and the student's individual needs. Students with an autism spectrum diagnosis are all different and have different strengths and needs. The topics Eric and I chose to discuss will not necessarily be the same choices other families will make. When considering what to talk about with the student, remember that it is often not the academics that are most challenging for students on the autism spectrum. Students may need some help with academic strategies, but there are also many details of daily life at college that can prove challenging for students. Some basic but important aspects of daily life on campus that may create difficulties include managing money, navigating the campus, getting help at the library, using an alarm clock, following dormitory rules, and finding meals to eat on campus. The list of possible topics is extensive so the parents and the student should choose those areas to discuss that might be the most problematic for the student. It is not difficult to then develop written guidelines, checklists, or whatever is appropriate to help the student understand what is ahead of them. When to begin these discussions will also vary. I recommend not waiting until the summer before going to college. Learning about life skills to help the student be more independent should start as early as possible. In this chapter I will explore some of the "lessons" Eric and I had and what we discussed.

Safety

Our first lesson was on safety, something very high on my personal list of priorities. All parents worry about their children's safety, especially if they are away from home. If you are a parent of a son or daughter on the autism spectrum you may be even more concerned with this issue. There are dangerous situations and strategies for staying safe that a student at college should know about. Since I couldn't teach Eric how to react in every possible dangerous situation, I tried to cover general safety tips and what he should do in emergencies. It was important to discuss with him a general strategy of what to do in *any* situation that felt wrong to him or made him scared. I suggested that Eric leave any place where he felt uncomfortable or didn't like what was going on around him. I told him he could call home whenever he felt he was in danger or in trouble, no matter what time it was. It is difficult to explain to someone what makes a situation dangerous. The best I could think of was to tell Eric to trust his feelings, and if it didn't feel right or he thought there were things going on that were wrong or possibly illegal, he should get away from the situation or seek help.

In our discussion about safety we talked about being safe walking at night on campus—staying near groups of people rather than walking alone, staying near lit areas, and avoiding empty dark parking garages or alleys. We talked about what situations might necessitate using the emergency call boxes on campus. We also discussed staying safe in the dormitory room—keeping the door locked at night and finding out who is at the door before letting them in. We talked about how easy it can be to steal a laptop computer and steps Eric could take to keep his computer from getting stolen. Safety on the computer is also an important issue to discuss with the college student. Students need to realize the dangers of giving out personal information on the internet or in chat rooms. This can be an especially complicated issue for students on the autism spectrum who may have difficulties identifying what may be a threat when the online world seems so impersonal.

For students who live at home and commute to school on public transportation there are other safety issues to consider. The student may need to learn how to ride a bus or subway and what dangers to be alert for when waiting at bus or train stops. A student should also know what to do if someone comes up to them and asks for money and how they can react to strangers who may talk to them. Some students on the autism spectrum may be highly vulnerable and unaware of the possibility of people taking advantage of them.

An important issue to discuss with any student going to college is what procedure to follow if there is an emergency. The terrorist attack of 9/11 happened while Eric was at school. There was also a severe ice storm later that same year causing widespread power outages in the area. Neither situation required Eric to evacuate but it made me realize that he needed a plan about who to contact or where to go. We made a list of all the phone numbers he might need for emergencies—health services, the campus police, his resident advisor for his hall, and all of his family members' phone numbers. I also knew that every dormitory requires fire drills to show students how to evacuate the building if there is an emergency. I reminded Eric to pay close attention to the procedure they ask students to follow. Unfortunately, dormitories may have fire drills in the middle of the night. The student should be warned of the possibility of this happening and discuss strategies they can use to stay calm.

Health issues

Teaching someone how to know when they are sick may seem way too basic for a student going to college. However, some students on the autism spectrum may need help in this area. Eric wasn't sure what symptoms someone has when they have a cold or the flu. We talked about what a normal body temperature should be and what to do if his temperature were higher than normal. He needed to learn what to do if he hurt himself, what constitutes an emergency and what does not, and where to go if he needs a doctor. We talked about the student health services on campus and how he could have routine visits to the doctor or nurse there for free. I also reminded Eric that if he needed help getting to the doctor that the school could supply medical escorts to Health Services if needed. We discussed basic first aid such as how to take care of a burn or cut. Describing what is an emergency and what is not was harder to explain. I tried to think of situations Eric might experience and described them and the best ways to react. Most important, I reminded Eric that he could call us or the resident advisor in the dormitory whenever he wasn't sure what to do.

As part of this lesson we put together a simple first aid kit with the basic items he would need. We included a thermometer, bandages, and antibacterial ointment as well as some medicines such as ibuprofen, nausea medicine, and cold and cough medicine. I showed Eric how to read the directions on the medicines and suggested he always write down the time he took a dose so that he could keep track of how often he was taking it. I wasn't confident that he could handle all of this independently so I encouraged him to call me when he felt sick so that we could talk about what he should do. The Health Services office on college campuses can be a good resource for students if they have medical questions or concerns. They may also offer courses for students on different topics related to health issues.

Many students on the autism spectrum may have medical issues that require medications. The student may need written instructions for all medications and a schedule of when to take them. The student should also keep a list of their medications and the prescribed dosages in the room and on their person in case that information is needed by Health Services or if there is a medical emergency.

Academic issues

Eric and I met twice during the summer before college to talk about academic issues. We talked about how to study for exams. A student on the autism spectrum may sometimes have difficulty knowing what is most important in a chapter or in a lecture. Eric and I looked at a textbook together and I pointed out the highlighted words and definitions and the review sections at the end of the chapters. I reminded Eric that he would own his college textbooks, unlike in high school, and that he could highlight or underline important parts of the chapters as he studied. If the textbook for a class was bought used, he should not assume another student's underlined or highlighted words were correct and he should use his own. We talked about how to choose what material to study—class notes, textbook information, lab notes, etc. and how to tell what the professor might include in the exam. We discussed basic organizational strategies for studying: beginning studying several days before a test, using note cards for important facts, rereading important chapters, and how to "cram" right before an exam.

One academic issue that may be challenging for some students on the autism spectrum is working on group projects. Eric had always preferred to work independently if possible and high school teachers would sometimes allow him to do so instead of working with a group of students. We knew that Eric would most likely not have that option in college. We talked about what working in groups felt like to Eric, and what he liked and didn't like about it. We then discussed ways to work with people who might have different ideas and the importance of each student being responsible for their own contribution to the group project. The organizational aspect of arranging meetings with other students was something I thought might also be challenging for Eric. I suggested that Eric keep a written list of the students he would be working with, including their e-mail addresses or phone numbers, and that he write down any scheduled meeting times in his calendar.

It is often difficult for a student to know when they need additional academic help. Eric needed some guidelines to make this judgment. I suggested that he consider talking to the instructor if he scored below a grade C on a test. I also encouraged him to contact an instructor whenever he didn't understand new information introduced in class. Knowing when help is needed is not going to be clear-cut in most situations. The student will most likely have to learn how to judge their academic needs through their experiences in college courses.

We also discussed where to go for help with academic issues. I told Eric that the instructor would always be the first person he should go to when he had questions or didn't understand the material. He could also talk to his service provider at Disabilities Services about difficulties he was having in a class. She could help him clarify the problem and also direct him to where he could go for more help if needed. We talked about the tutoring office on campus and how to access a tutor. Eric and I also discussed study groups and how they could possibly be helpful to him. I encouraged him to join any study groups he could because they would help him with the academic work and also give him the opportunity to get to know other students.

Taking notes during a college lecture can be difficult for students on the autism spectrum. Some students, like Eric, may have fine motor weaknesses that affect the speed at which they can write. Students also may have difficulty understanding what the important information is that needs to be written down. It can help the student if the instructor announces the important points as he makes them or emphasizes the information that may be on the next test. This won't always happen, however, and the student must have some ability to do this independently. Unless they have had specific instruction in this area, the student may not actually know how to take good notes. When Eric was in high school I discovered he was writing lecture notes in complete sentences. He was not aware of the importance of abbreviating his notes or of how to make an outline of important facts. Parents may want to look at an example of the student's note taking and see if they could benefit from some instruction on ways to improve this skill. There are accommodations available to help students with this issue that will be discussed more in Chapter 5.

Self-help skills

The category of self-help skills encompasses many different aspects of a student's daily life. It includes basic necessary skills such as setting an alarm to wake up in the morning, maintaining good personal hygiene, dressing appropriately for the weather, and finding food to eat. Some students on the autism spectrum may have wonderful skills in this area and be able independently to take care of all their personal needs but some students may need strategies to guide them. Hygiene can be a difficult area because it involves the student making an assessment of how they look, which is challenging for some students on the autism spectrum. The way a student looks (or smells) can directly influence how others react to them, so good hygiene can play an important part in developing a social network. During one of our meetings Eric and I discussed the importance of regularly shaving and showering and using deodorant. Rather than relying on Eric's ability to judge whether he needs to shave, it is easier for him to have a regular schedule for shaving.

Clothing selection can also be a challenge for some students on the autism spectrum. Of course, knowing how to dress appropriately for the weather seems to be a challenge for all college students. Walk around any college campus on a cold day and I guarantee that you will see students walking to class in shorts or short-sleeved shirts. Eric does a good job determining how to dress for the weather conditions and if he misjudges how cool or warm it is outdoors, he will typically change his clothes to something more appropriate. Choosing clothes that match or go together can be more of a challenge for Eric. To make it easier to match his clothes, Eric has always owned neutral color pants or blue jeans that will coordinate with any of his shirts. He has no distinct preference for the kind of clothes he wears in terms of color, brand, or style. What is most important to Eric is that the clothing is comfortable. We therefore try to shop for the comfortable clothing he likes at stores that are popular with his age group so that Eric's clothing will fit with what other individuals his age wear.

I knew one big adjustment for Eric in college was going to be sharing a bathroom with other students in his dormitory. He would not have the privacy he was accustomed to. With only one shower available, he would also have to decide when would be the most convenient time to shower that would fit his schedule and the schedule of other students on his hall. We talked during our lesson about what sharing a bathroom would be like. It was important that he know ahead of time what some of the issues might be so he could prepare for them.

Like some individuals with autism, Eric has a very limited diet of foods he will eat. I knew he would not be able to find most of these foods in the dining halls on campus. He would need to have his favorite foods in his dorm room and eat most of his meals there. Together we made a list of all the food and paper products he would need to have meals in his room during the week. He could keep this list on his computer, make changes if needed, and print it out to take with him to the grocery store to use as a shopping list. This way he would not have to rewrite it each time and could just mark off the items he didn't need that week.

We also talked during this lesson about the places to eat on campus that might serve foods Eric likes and where they were located. The student may also need to know the hours when meals are provided at dining halls and the hours of operation for the fast food restaurants on campus. This information is important when the student chooses their class schedule and has to factor in where and when they can fit a meal between classes. For students with more typical eating habits, parents will need to discuss the importance of healthy eating and how the student can make good choices. Most colleges try to offer healthy choices but many parents of college students are dismayed by the amount of "junk food" their son or daughter eats.

The university Eric attends has a wonderful "cash-less" plan for students. All the student needs to have is their student identification card or ID to buy food at campus restaurants and dining halls. The students have accounts where money can be deposited for the school year and the student ID serves almost as a debit card for making purchases. Students can also use this account and their ID to pay for making copies at the library or for food items from vending machines and convenience stores on campus. This is a great plan for students with autism spectrum disorders who may have difficulties with purchases. It also keeps them from having to be responsible for carrying around cash all the time. Many universities are providing this service to students on campus and parents might want to explore this option.

Most dormitories on campus have laundry facilities for students to use. Many have coin operated machines, and Eric's university also has the "cashless" way of paying with the student ID as described above. A college student may need instruction on how to use the machines and the basic directions on how to wash clothes. Teaching the student at home is helpful but it would be more useful if the student could learn at the actual laundry facility they will be using. Written directions on how much detergent to use, how to separate lights from darks, etc., could be used by the student to help them do their laundry independently. Because Eric comes home fairly frequently, he helps with his laundry at home and doesn't use the laundry at school. Not all students will have that luxury, however, so parents may need to teach this skill to the student.

There are many steps a student must be able to do independently in order to get to a class on time. They must be able to estimate how much time they will need to get ready before class and set the appropriate time on an alarm clock to wake them up. For many students, this can be difficult. It helped Eric to have the experience of using an alarm clock during high school. I recommend to parents that they start getting the student used to this as early as possible. Many students have difficulty judging how much time they will need in the morning to get ready. You can practice this too during high school, timing how long it takes the student to get completely ready to go in the morning. If the student tends to be especially slow-moving in the morning, any preparation they can do the night before can help. They can select the clothes they will wear or pack their book bag the night before. When Eric and I discussed this during one of our meetings, we estimated how much time it normally took him in high school to get ready and added in how much time it would take him to walk to class. We then added some extra time so that he wouldn't be anxious about being late and could be early to class if he wanted to find a good seat. Parents may need to talk to the student fairly frequently during the first couple of weeks of classes to find out how this is going. They may also need to help the student adjust their schedules if they are finding themselves consistently late to class.

Time management

One of the most difficult areas for any new student in college is knowing how to use their time wisely: when to play and when to work. Students must decide ahead of time how long it will take to do a particular assignment and then choose when to start working on it to have it completed on time. The student must also judge the importance of the assignment or test in reference to how they are doing in that particular class or how important the course is for their major. Students must also choose the place and time of the day that are most conducive to studying. Does the student study better in the evening or during the day? Would they get more accomplished in their room or at the library?

Students may be able to judge how important the assignment is and when they should be working on it, but can they make themselves do the work when they have so many other temptations and fun choices around them? There is no Mom or Dad around to remind them of their responsibilities. Instructors don't remind them of upcoming due dates for assignments. It is all up to the student. This is hard for all students, especially those on the autism spectrum.

The temptations for students on the spectrum may be different than for other students. Many students may want to spend more time doing independent activities related to their special interests. They may like reading books about their interests or going online on the computer and searching for information about their interests. They may be less distracted by the parties in their dormitory or attending sporting events. No matter what their individual choices might be, the student has to have the ability to "see the whole picture" and understand their responsibilities as a student.

The first thing Eric and I did during our lesson on time management was talk about things he could do for fun at college. For people on the autism spectrum work is frequently more like play and play is often more difficult. Down time or unstructured time can be difficult for students on the autism spectrum. It was important for Eric to know what his free time choices might be. I also thought it might help him to make a written list of activities he could do on campus that he could refer to if needed. The process of making this list together also gave us the opportunity to talk about what he enjoys and all the possibilities that would be available to him at college. It gave him things to look forward to and helped to relieve some of the anxiety he might have been feeling about the transition.

Eric wrote down the ideas as we both contributed suggestions. It was difficult at the beginning for Eric to think of activities because of his lack of experience on a college campus. He didn't have a clear idea of what the options would be. I started the conversation with a couple of ideas I thought would interest Eric—going to the library to read books about animals and going to the large park located near campus. Eric liked both suggestions and wrote them on the list. He then started making suggestions and together we ended up with quite a few good ideas. I doubt he had to refer to this list once he was at college, but the act of writing it was helpful and made him less worried about the transition.

When having this discussion with the student it is important to think about activities both on and off campus. It is helpful to include activities that are free or low cost because many students in college are on a tight budget. For all students on the autism spectrum, even those students who typically prefer being alone, it is important to include activities the student can do with others. Many of these students will want to have social outlets with their peers and it can help to have some ideas of possible activities. After the student transitions to college they may still need some guidance in locating extra-curricular activities. Parents can occasionally ask the student if they are bored or if they would like help finding activities on campus.

Making a list of fun things Eric could do was the easy part. Explaining how to manage his time between school work and fun was not as easy.

My son is very rule oriented and we talked about the rules and responsibilities of all students in college—what the school expects from the students, what instructors or professors expect from the students, and what we as his parents expect from Eric. There are distinct rules concerning the grade point average students must maintain to avoid academic suspension or possible expulsion from school. Eric and I also discussed how college is a choice and a privilege. By the end of our discussion, Eric knew what his responsibilities would be to the school and to us. He had a better understanding of why fulfilling the requirements of his courses should be his first priority.

The resource notebook

The list of possible activities for free time and any written information from our "lessons" during the summer were included in a resource notebook for Eric. When they first enter college and during orientation, students are given an incredible amount of information including forms, announcements, and a list of rules. A resource notebook can be a good strategy for any student as a way to keep the important information in one location. Among other things, I included articles we read about college issues, first aid information, a list of restaurant and food services on campus and their location, and information about the computer services on campus. Parents can organize the notebook in any way that works for the student. In Eric's notebook I included the following sections: Contacts, Academics, Disability Services, Financial, Housing, Dining, Technology, and Leisure.

Probably the most important and most used section of Eric's resource notebook is Contacts. In this section we put a list of all the people and offices Eric might need to contact while at school. Included is a list of Eric's family members, their phone numbers—work, home, and cell—and their e-mail addresses. Also included on this list are family friends located nearby and their numbers in case there is an emergency and Eric can't reach a family member. Other emergency numbers are included such as the campus police and the student health center. This section also includes a list of individuals on campus whom Eric may need to contact such as his service provider at Disabilities Services, his resident advisor, and his academic advisor. Contact information for other important offices at the university such as Counseling Services, Computer Services, Housing, and Career Counseling is included in this section as well.

The Academics section of the resource notebook includes a variety of information. Besides the contact information for his academic advisor, it includes any correspondence from the department of his major. Eric received an introduction to the department explaining the student and faculty responsibilities, the curriculum guidelines for the department, curriculum requirements for his major, and a list of the general education electives students may choose from. Much of this information can also be found on the university's website. In addition to a list of general requirements for the major, I also included in the Academics section Eric's current schedule of classes. Following his first semester in college, I added an updated record of his progress towards his major, what courses he had taken and the grades he had received, and what courses he had yet to take to satisfy the requirements of his major. This information can also be easily accessed on the university website.

The third section in Eric's resource notebook we labeled Disability Services. This section may have a different name depending on what the school calls the support services for students. Some students may be more comfortable referring to it without the word "disability" in the title. Whatever is understandable and appropriate for the individual student is best. In this section the student would keep any information needed for accessing services for support through the school. General information about the office would be important to include, such as the names of the staff and contact information, the hours the office is open, and a list of any other services offered within that building that may be appropriate. Counseling services and tutoring services may also be located within the Disabilities Services building. In Eric's notebook we included a copy of his Services and Accommodations Agreement signed by Eric and his service provider. This is the letter of agreement stating the accommodations Eric qualifies for. This form will need to be updated if the accommodations change. We also added a description of each accommodation Eric would be receiving including the process of accessing each one. This information should be available on the university's website or at the Disabilities Services office.

The Financial section of the resource notebook contains information about Eric's checking account and bank card and locations of ATM machines on campus. It also includes tutorial information from the bank that describes how to read a bank statement, how to write a check, and how to write a deposit slip. It may be helpful also to include in this section the contact information for the Financial Aid office or any information on loans the student receives. Eric receives financial aid from our county VR office and that information is also kept in this section of his resource notebook.

Information about housing and dining are also included in the notebook. The Housing section may include the student's housing assignment notification, any rules or procedures for that particular dormitory, and reminder information about when and how to sign up for housing for the following year. This section could also hold any notices the student receives about upcoming dormitory meetings or parties. The Dining section of Eric's resource notebook contains a map showing all the dining halls as well as the convenience stores and fast food restaurants on campus. It is helpful to include the hours of service for each dining facility. Eric also has a printout of his grocery list in this section of the notebook. If the student has a prepaid meal plan with the university, information about that can be kept in this section.

The Technology section contains any information about the computer services on campus, how to contact them, how to report a problem, and where to take the system for repair. It also contains a list of computer labs on campus. This section of the resource notebook also includes information about the telecommunications on campus, the cable television service, and the long distance telephone service. In Eric's notebook we included a list of the cable channels and the number to call to report a problem with the cable service. We also included a list of the telephone options and the dialing instructions for using the different options. Most of this information is given to college students when they sign up for services or when they first move into the dormitory.

The last section in Eric's resource notebook we called Leisure. It is where Eric put his list of things to do during his free time. We also included the telephone number for a local movie theater and video rental store. Most colleges have various clubs on campus addressing different areas of interest. You can typically find information about the different clubs or organizations available on the school website or in packets of information given to new students. We included information in Eric's notebook about two clubs he might be interested in. If the student enjoys sporting events, concerts, or plays this would be a good place to keep schedules for games or events.

To complete Eric's resource notebook we added a map of campus and a campus bus schedule. These are typically available at many locations on campus. We also added all of Eric's own contact information in the front of the notebook—his social security number, his school mailing address and e-mail address, and his phone number. Eric didn't know this information at the beginning of college, and it helped to have it written down and easily accessible. As I mentioned before, what we decided to put in Eric's notebook might be different from what someone else might choose to include. What is most important is that the notebook include whatever the student might need to remember or refer to for help, and that it should be kept in one place that is easily accessible. Parents may also want to start a notebook like this earlier than the summer right before the transition to college. A notebook could be started in high school and include information helpful in choosing a college or the student's progress in high school towards graduation.

Orientation

Much of the information for the resource notebook came from the school orientation we attended. Orientation is not only helpful to the students but can also be extremely helpful to parents, especially parents of students with disabilities. Most schools offer an orientation for freshmen at some point before school starts. Orientation may take place during the first few days of the school year, or it may be offered during the summer. There is a wealth of information shared during orientation, and parents of students on the autism spectrum should participate if at all possible. At our particular university, the orientation was two days long and was for both students and parents. Students stayed on campus in a dormitory. This orientation was for all incoming new students. Some colleges may offer separate orientations through the Disabilities Services support office specifically for new students with disabilities.

The benefits of orientation for students on the autism spectrum are many. The student gets to experience what it is like to live in a dormitory room at least for one evening. (At Eric's university we were able to request that he have a room to himself for orientation.) Spending a night in a dormitory room during orientation gave him an experience that helped prepare him for moving into the dormitory in the fall.

Orientation provides the opportunity for students to become familiar with campus. There were tours of campus for all the incoming freshmen and visits to several important offices providing services to students. Eric and I were also able to walk his class schedule during orientation to find the classroom buildings and rooms where his classes would be located. As in all the previous years of public school, it was helpful for Eric to "practice" his schedule beforehand.

Another advantage of orientation for students is being able to hear about other students' experiences. Eric's orientation included a panel of upperclassmen, junior and senior students, who talked to students about their experiences. They talked about what was fun about college and what was difficult. They talked about being homesick and some of the mistakes they made during their freshman year. They gave specific strategies for using time wisely and for finding a quiet place to study. All of this information was great for Eric to hear and especially meaningful because it was coming from his peers.

There were several social events planned for students during the orientation and, much to my surprise, Eric attended most of them. There was a dodge ball game, a dance, and a mock "Dating Game" show. A goal of the orientation was to make the student feel like part of a team. They showed students that they are not alone if they feel nervous about coming to college and being on their own. The social events during orientation were also great opportunities for Eric to meet other students while at the same time learning what being in college is like.

As I mentioned earlier, orientation can also be very beneficial for parents. As a parent of a child with a disability, it was especially helpful to me to be around parents of "typical" students. I could see that they had some of the same concerns I did. I was definitely not the only parent worried about their child leaving home. I also learned at orientation how accessible the instructors would be for Eric if he needed them. This was a concern for me because of the size of the university and the large number of students. With e-mail it has become much easier to communicate. The instructors also offer regular office hours where they can meet with students on a one-to-one basis.

Part of our orientation for parents involved demonstrating some of the technologies used on campus. Just about everything is done now on the computer, from signing up for classes to paying for meals. Many instructors have their own websites where they list assignments and post lecture notes. On some instructors' websites students complete homework and have it corrected and graded almost immediately. All this advanced technology makes it easier for the students on the autism spectrum, who may do better on the computer than when speaking with people in person. Many of the processes for signing up for classes, housing, cable TV, etc., were demonstrated to parents during orientation. It was helpful to know how to do these things so I could be available to Eric if he had difficulty with any of these processes.

One of the most helpful parts of orientation for me personally wasn't given during a meeting or tour or support group. It was a seemingly trivial experience that had a major impact on me. Eric attended a dance during orientation for the incoming freshmen. At the dance Eric won a prize for "Best Male Dancer." The next day when I said, "Eric, I didn't even know you could dance!" he said, "I didn't either. I've never danced before in my life." The prize he won was a water bottle with the school emblem on it and it meant more to me than a huge trophy or a big cash prize. It represented to me the hope that other college students would accept Eric for who he is and that he would be OK. It was an incredible gift.

5 Adjusting to the Move

Adjusting to the move to college can be difficult for any student. Patty Carlton in her article "Transitioning into the Residence Hall" says, "Let's face it, for most students living at home is a 'piece of cake.' There is laundry service, food service, built-in financial aid assistance, maid service, space for solitude, usually a private room with a personal closet and a chest of drawers, entertainment equipment, etc. Dorm life has none of these advantages" (Carlton 1998, p.6).

It can also be a difficult adjustment for a parent to send their child to college. It's a very emotional experience and when that child also happens to have a disability, the emotions can be even more intense. I was struggling with the conflicting feelings I was having, pride in what my son had been able to accomplish and fear for his safety. I was so happy for him and so sad about his going. At times I felt confident that he would do well and at other times I just knew he would fail. I knew that this next stage in Eric's life was going to be a huge adjustment for Eric, but also for me as his mother.

I spent a great deal of time before the move to the dorm thinking about the earlier years with Eric and how far he had come. Though the details of the memories sometimes blurred, I could still remember how hard it was for him at different times in his life. Despite all of that or maybe because of that, Eric had grown into a wonderful young man with his own distinct and very likable personality. He was now adding to our lives and the lives of others in ways I never could have imagined. Eric, without meaning to, became a sort of "poster child" in our local community of autism. When other parents of younger children on the autism spectrum would hear that Eric was going to college their eyes would light up (and sometimes well up) as they saw hope for their own child.

Eric was never aware of the effect his story had on other people. I would occasionally tell him about other parents or teachers who were inspired by what he had accomplished and it always seemed to surprise him. He didn't feel as if he had done anything special. His acceptance of himself helped to remind me that I needed to think of Eric as a student going to college, not a student with autism going to college. But when I thought about Eric in comparison to the "typical" freshman going to college, I was scared. I knew it was going to be a challenge for him to perform many of the basic tasks of daily living at college. The feelings of pride for all he had accomplished were sometimes overpowered by doubts and concerns about the things I wasn't sure he could do. These competing emotions only added to the stress I felt about the upcoming moving day.

Eric did not seem anxious at all. He was excited more than anything else. We had made a conscious effort to build up this experience as something that would be fun and special in his life and he wasn't worried about it at all. This may not be the case for many students on the autism spectrum who are transitioning to college. Parents should probably expect this transition to be difficult for the student. Change is typically very hard for individuals on the autism spectrum no matter how much preparation has been done. To help the student who is feeling anxious, parents can encourage them to talk about or write down their feelings. They may need to visit the campus several times or talk to someone else who has made the transition before. Whatever strategy is chosen to help the student with their anxiety, parents need to be especially attentive to the student's feelings about the move.

Anyone who has ever moved a child to college knows how much work has to be done ahead of time. There are many items that have to be purchased—clothes, bath supplies, school supplies, bedding, etc. Most colleges will give incoming freshmen a list of items they will need to bring on move-in day. These checklists are very helpful. If you have trouble finding a checklist, make one with the student and use it to gather the items needed. The actual process of checking off each thing as you collect it can reduce stress for the student. The student should be involved with purchasing these items and making the choices for his or her room. Even if students don't seem to care about the colors of sheets or towels, they should still be involved in making the choices. They need to feel ownership for their new environment. I found that while Eric was preparing for college he showed more interest in buying clothes and personal items than he had ever done before. Buying the items for the dorm room can also give the student practice writing checks or using a credit card. This experience will prepare them for the financial responsibilities they will have in college.

One of the most important items that may be purchased for a student going to college is a computer. Many colleges are now requiring freshmen students to have a computer when they arrive at school. Internet access is available in most college dormitory rooms. Some colleges do not require a student to have their own computer but instead provide computer facilities for students. For all college students, but especially for a student on the autism spectrum, it is probably best if they do have their own computer. That way the student can become familiar with using their own computer and they don't have to worry about locating a computer center and finding a computer that is open at the times they need to use one. Most schools will give recommendations to incoming students about what features the computer should have.

If the student is going to purchase their own computer, they must decide whether to buy a laptop computer or a desktop computer. There are several factors to be considered in making this decision. Laptop computers are typically more expensive than desktop computers and may be more expensive to repair. They are more vulnerable to damage, since they can be accidentally dropped, and are more vulnerable to theft. Laptops are generally less capable than desktop computers and may have limited upgrade possibilities. On the positive side, most laptops have more than enough features and performance to meet the needs of a college student. Their portability is a significant advantage because it allows them to be used in a variety of places. They can be taken to classes, to the library, or to other areas on campus where students gather to study. Laptops also require less space than a desktop computer, which can be an advantage in a small dormitory room. We chose to buy a laptop computer for Eric and it has served his needs well. It has been helpful that he can bring it with him when he comes home on weekends or for breaks from school. Families and students will need to weigh the benefits of both kinds of computer and purchase what is most appropriate for the individual student.

As you begin to collect the various items to take to college you need to find a way to organize and store them until moving day. There are many kinds of inexpensive containers that can be bought to store the items, and they can be stacked in an out-of-the-way place until needed. The kinds of containers that can fit under a bed are especially useful. Because space is limited in a dorm room these containers can also be used later in the room to hold extra sheets or towels. Plastic waterproof containers are also great for a rainy moving day.

It is important to many students to bring some of their "comfort" items from home to the dorm. When I drove Eric back to college after his first weekend home I asked him if he was looking forward to going back to school. He answered, "Of course. My stuff is there." Eric's favorite things are books and videos or DVDs. Before the move he picked out his favorite books and movies, those he couldn't live without, to take with him to college. Deciding what is indispensable can be very difficult when the student is so accustomed to having all of their things together, and parents may have to help the student decide. I encouraged Eric to leave some favorite books and videos at home so he could look forward to seeing them when he comes home for visits. If you are expecting the student to come home regularly you don't want to remove all the items that make home comforting to them.

Every college is going to have its own process to follow on move-in day, but most will try to make the task as easy as possible. They often stagger the students across several days to keep the numbers manageable. They may offer "helpers" at each dorm to help carry items to the room. The process for getting the key to the room and signing in is sometimes confusing. At our school the student goes to a designated place at the dorm to sign in and pick up their room key. They must check the room over for any problems, including missing or damaged items. The student then fills out a form verifying the condition of the room and gives it to the resident advisor.

Resident advisors, or RAs, are fellow students and are usually upper-classmen. RAs typically live on the same hall or very near to the students they advise. They frequently receive free or reduced room-and-board in exchange for taking on some responsibilities in the dormitory. An RA is specially trained to help students, and can serve as a peer advisor or a resource person for the other students on the hall. The RAs are chosen by academic achievement, a general knowledge of the campus resources, strong social and verbal skills, and an overall willingness and interest in helping other students. The RA may be the first person the new student will need to go to if there is a problem in the room or if they have questions. If the RA doesn't know the answers to your questions, they will know how to help the student find the answers. This individual can play an important role in the student's life at college and parents will most likely want to meet this person on move-in day.

Many students buy their textbooks on the day they move into the dorm. Unless the college has a free textbook service, the textbooks are very expensive and parents may need to be there with the student to pay for the books. The books for one semester can average around $300 or more. Parents may also want to be available to help the student find all the required books. Some colleges or universities may offer a way for students to "pre-order" their textbooks. During the summer, the student can sign up for this option and the bookstore gets the student's schedule, gathers the textbooks for each class, and packages them together for the student to pick up before classes start. It saves time walking down crowded aisles with hundreds of other students looking for the right textbook for a particular class. I recommend to parents that they use this service if it is available at their college because it makes for one less thing to do on the busy moving day.

Eric's moving day was unbelievably hard. Not only was it physically exhausting carrying load after load up two flights of stairs and putting together book cases (bring a toolbox!), but the air conditioning was not working in the dorm and it felt like an oven in his room. I have distinct memories of my husband sitting at Eric's desk trying to get his computer working and looking like he had taken a shower with his clothes on. Eric handled it very well and with no grumbling at all, unlike the rest of us. He was so excited to be there that he didn't care that it was 100 degrees in his room.

It's helpful if parents are available to stay on moving day and help unpack and put things away. However, parents may need to fight the urge to decide where to put everything. That should be the student's decision. The student will need to participate in putting things in drawers so they will be able to find things later. I think our staying for a little while after moving Eric in may have helped him adjust to the move. I know it helped me. We used that time to help Eric get settled in, meet some of the other students in his dormitory, and walk around campus with him as he explored his new surroundings. Parents should be sensitive to what the student prefers of course. Parents may want to ask the student whether they would like them to leave or stay for a while.

I cried all the way home from campus that day. I was overwhelmed with all the emotions I had kept under control all day. When my husband and I were alone for the first time in the car, the flood gates opened. I know I was crying for all the typical reasons parents cry when they send their child to college. I was sad about leaving Eric knowing how much I would miss him. I was also sad about having to let go, knowing that Eric had reached a new stage of independence from us. I knew our life would never be the same. I was crying too because I was worried. I was worried about whether we had made the right decision and whether Eric would be OK. But there were tears of joy too, tears of celebration for all that Eric had accomplished and how far he had come. For many years I hadn't allowed myself to dream that this day would ever come and here it was and the future was full of hope.

Part of my adjustment to letting go and allowing Eric to be more independent involved the change in my role in advocating for Eric. For 15 years I had been the primary advocate for him at school. I was the behind-the-scenes director to make sure he got all the services he needed. I made sure people understood what Eric was not able to explain himself. Eric, like many other individuals on the autism spectrum, frequently did not fit the mold. With children as unique as ours, parents often have to strongly advocate not only for the resources to help them, but for the acceptance of the student. Through most of his school career the people working with Eric were not trained in autism. It was often necessary for me to help educate the teachers about the spectrum and about Eric's individual strengths and needs.

One of the most important things we can do as parents is to help individuals on the autism spectrum learn to advocate for themselves. The first step can be to help the child understand his or her differences and strengths and weaknesses. We start this process when our child is young, maybe when we first talk to them about their differences from others. How we explain this and how we react to their disability will influence their own acceptance of their autism or Asperger Syndrome. If we accept their differences and treasure our children for who they are, they will, we hope, feel better about themselves.

The better students feel about themselves, the more comfortable they will feel when asking for accommodations in college. Involvement in IEP meetings at school, especially in the high school years, can give the student experience in talking to others about their needs and strengths. It also educates the student about the services that are available to help people learn. Another way parents can help the student be a better self-advocate is by helping them understand that all students have different learning needs. They may not realize that many college students, for a variety of reasons or disabilities, need accommodations to help with learning. The majority of students receiving accommodations in colleges are students with learning disabilities. It is not unusual to have a student in a class who needs a note taker or needs to tape record lectures. Parents can remind the student on the autism spectrum that they are not alone in needing some help to be successful in college.

Any college student who is 18 or older and is their own guardian must speak up for themselves and make decisions for themselves. Legally, the service providers cannot share information about a student with the parents unless the student directly requests them to do so. They will not contact parents when there is a problem unless it is an emergency and they will not ask parents for information about the student. Parents are not typically invited to meetings. The student has to be able to go to the office on campus where the services are located, initiate a request for services, and follow through on the process of obtaining these services. If the student is embarrassed about their disability or self-conscious about needing help it can interfere with their abilities to self-advocate.

My role after Eric moved into the dormitory became more one of supporting from afar. I no longer knew the day-to-day goings-on in his life. I wasn't there to problem solve with him when he had difficulty or give him ideas or strategies. From now on he was going to have to immediately solve problems on his own or ask someone else on campus to help him. Luckily Eric still values my opinions and listens to my suggestions. He will call me if he can't solve a problem on his own or when he has a question. I encourage parents to remind students that although they are adults and responsible for themselves now, they can still come to you for help if they need it or for emotional support if things get overwhelming. Asking questions or sharing concerns does not make them less independent or less capable.

I don't know how Eric felt during the first few weeks after moving into the dormitory. He would never tell me about any of his feelings during this time. I asked him sometimes if he was having fun and he always said yes. I asked if his classes were difficult and he said no. We talked every other day on the phone the first few weeks. I had warned him before the move that I would need to talk to him frequently the first week or two to make sure everything was going OK. I always had to call him—he never called home—but he always seemed happy to hear from me. This was a time when it definitely helped to ask the right questions because Eric was not being very forthcoming about how the transition was going. I was careful not to ask too much about his personal life but asked more about how his classes were going. He would occasionally ask me where something was in his room that we had unpacked but he couldn't find or ask questions about his cable television or computer service.

The first few days he was at school I struggled with not knowing what he was doing and whether he was OK. I know I must have driven my husband crazy because I was always asking him, "I wonder how Eric is doing?" The umbilical cord still felt attached and I had to really control myself not to drive over to the university to see him. My husband and my friends were very supportive during this time. What helped the most was having frequent communication with Eric. Sometimes all I needed was to hear his voice. Staying busy also helped me: I would be distracted from thinking about him so much.

The first home visit after moving to the dorm room is important, especially for the parent. As a mother it was very important for me to see my son, touch him, make sure he was OK, and of course feed him his favorite foods. I now understand this need of mothers to feed their children when they come home. Maybe we use food to remind them of how much they need us or maybe to remind ourselves of how much we are needed! Seeing Eric that first weekend home and being able to ask him more about school was important to my surviving his transition to college. Every subsequent visit home made it a little easier emotionally.

I remember the first time I realized I had gone a whole day without thinking about how Eric was doing at school. I felt guilty about it and that I would be letting him down somehow if I didn't think about him all the time and worry about what was happening to him. This is probably a fairly common reaction for parents as they adjust to letting go. As more days went by when I didn't need to worry about Eric, I got over the guilt and learned to appreciate not having to be so involved in my son's life. Every parent is going to have their own reaction to this transition and there is no right way to get through it.

As I write this, it has been over three years since we left Eric at college for the first time. I was recently on campus for a meeting to hear about career options for individuals with disabilities. As I was walking from the parking deck to the building where the meeting was, I noticed students walking to classes and I looked for Eric. I would have been happy to see him but I knew I probably wouldn't. When I left campus to come home following the meeting it struck me that I wasn't taking Eric something he needed or stopping by to check on him. I hadn't seen him in almost two weeks but that was OK because I knew I would see him soon. I had come a long way since the move-in day.

6 Supports and Strategies in College

Lars Perner, a college professor and individual with Asperger Syndrome, said in his presentation at the Autism Society of America's Annual Conference in 2002, "For many high-functioning individuals on the autistic spectrum, college can be about as close as you can get to Heaven on Earth" (Perner 2002, p.2). Some individuals on the autism spectrum may agree with Dr. Perner while others may have very different stories to tell. For students with any kind of disability, the transition to college often means the loss of the support systems that have been helping guide their daily lives for years. How successful or how enjoyable the college experience can be will often depend on the student's ability to develop a new support system in college.

The student who has an autism spectrum disorder may have difficulties in a variety of areas when transitioning to college. They may have problems with organizational issues such as attending classes or completing assignments on time. Students may fail to realize when they are having academic difficulty and, when they do, they may have problems communicating with the instructors. Socially, students on the autism spectrum may have difficulty initiating conversations with other students. Every college student's experience will be different and will require different levels of support.

Section 504 of the Rehabilitation Act of 1973 is the legislation that mandates that colleges and universities provide equal access to programs and services for students with and without disabilities. According to this law, any colleges or universities that receive federal financial assistance must not discriminate in the admission or treatment of students. Colleges may not limit the number of students with disabilities they accept and they cannot ask whether or not a student has a disability before admitting them. Colleges also may not exclude a student with a disability from a course of study and may not counsel a student toward pursuing a more restrictive career because of a disability. A student with a disability also may not be discriminated against in eligibility for financial assistance or internships or work-study programs (AHEAD 2004).

Parents and, if possible, the student should have a clear understanding of any laws that protect the rights of the student with a disability and the responsibilities expected from the instructors in providing these accommodations. In the United States, reasonable accommodations must be part of the instructional process to ensure equal educational opportunity. Students with disabilities should not have an advantage over others in class and class standards should not be lowered to accommodate the student. You should make yourself knowledgeable about the protections for students in college because you may find them quite different from the legal protections in public school.

If students at any point feel that they are being discriminated against by a college or university, they may contact the appropriate individual who handles these complaints. Some schools will have a Section 504 coordinator who coordinates the school's compliance with the law. The Disabilities Services coordinator should also be able to direct the student to the appropriate individual. The school must also have a grievance procedure that will include steps to making your complaint known. Most college handbooks or publications will include information about the grievance procedure (U.S. Department of Education, Office for Civil Rights 2002).

There are many supports available to students with disabilities at college. Most schools, whether they are smaller technical schools, or community colleges, or larger four-year private or state universities, will offer supports to students with a variety of disabilities. There are students who receive services in college for physical handicaps, chronic illnesses, hearing and visual impairments, epilepsy, mental retardation, and other disabilities. The majority of students who access supports are students with learning disabilities and/or attention deficit hyperactivity disorder

(ADHD). Many of the accommodations in college are helpful for a variety of learning needs including those of the student on the autism spectrum.

Parents are often surprised at the number of accommodations available at the college level. Many colleges or universities will offer extended time on tests and distraction-free settings for testing, as well as the use of computers for in-class writing assignments and tests that require writing. Other accommodations may include note takers or scribes, books on audio tape, priority registration for classes, priority seating in classes, and tape recording of lectures. Some schools may have classroom or academic assistants available for qualified students. These are all accommodations that can possibly benefit the student on the autism spectrum. Any accommodation a student receives is based on the documentation to support the need and is determined individually for each student. The accommodations chosen for the student at the beginning of college may be different during future years. The service provider and the student will usually review the need for accommodations each semester and make the decision based on the particular course and the student's current needs.

Colleges and universities require disability documentation that establishes that the student has a disability. The IEP from high school alone, or a prior history of receiving accommodations in school, does not automatically qualify a student for accommodations at the college level. The documentation concerning the disability must be current, usually within three years of enrollment in college. Each college sets its own standards and policies for the documentation that is required. The documentation that is usually required includes a diagnosis of the current disability, the credentials of the person making the diagnosis, the date of the diagnosis, and how that diagnosis was reached. It is also usually required that there be documentation on how the disability affects the life of the individual. In order to qualify for accommodations the documentation should show that a student currently has a "substantial limitation to a major life activity." The documentation must also show that the disability affects the student's ability to learn (U.S. Department of Education, Office for Civil Rights 2002).

In order to receive any accommodations, the student is responsible for supplying the testing results and documentation to the office of Disabilities Services. Colleges are not required to conduct the testing. The student should have received the testing needed during their final years of high school. If further testing is necessary, the student or the family may have to pay for it to be done privately. If the student is eligible for services through VR, they may be able to qualify for testing at no cost. You can locate your state VR agency through the Rehabilitative Services Administration (RSA) website listed in Appendix A.

Getting the documentation required may be more difficult for students who attend private secondary schools. In the public schools the student typically has evaluations done by the school that will be acceptable for college. Private schools normally do not require or provide evaluations, and parents will often need to hire someone privately to do the testing. It would be beneficial to explore the kind of documentation required at the colleges being considered before paying for evaluations that may not fit the college's criteria. In addition, students in private schools may not have received accommodations while in school and the college or university they attend may require documentation to prove the need for accommodations at the college level.

Different colleges will have different procedures for obtaining services. Parents and students need to research how to access services at each college or university they are considering. Disability services providers will be happy to meet with you and review the documentation required for services and the responsibilities of the student to obtain the needed accommodation. Pay close attention to the types of documentation that may be required, whom the reports should be coming from (physician, psychologist, psychiatrist, etc.) and how current the reports or testing should be. I frequently recommend to parents of students on the spectrum to take advantage of any testing offered through the school while the student is still in high school. That testing is typically free and often satisfies the current testing required at the college level. Colleges and universities may provide information on their websites about what is needed to access services and may even list the documentation necessary for individual disabilities.

A parent can help the student by learning about the actual procedure a student will need to go through to get accommodations. They can then discuss the procedure with the student before the transition to school.

Parents and the student can make a checklist of the steps the student is required to follow. At Eric's university, after submitting the necessary documentation the student schedules an appointment with Disability Services for Students (DSS) to discuss services and the student's limitations. The student then signs an Accommodations Agreement form for each semester that lists the accommodations they qualify for and will need.

The procedure for obtaining an accommodation in a particular class starts with the instructor being notified that the student is working with DSS and will need accommodations. At Eric's university a letter is written, with input from the student, and sent to each instructor who will be teaching the student that semester. The letter does not state the name of the disability, but instead describes briefly the effects the disability may have on the student's learning. This is important information for students who may be concerned about confidentiality issues. It has been my experience that the DSS office is very protective of the student's confidential information about their disability and no one can share this information except the student.

Eric's letters from DSS to his instructors state that his documented disability affects his ability to access certain activities, materials, and evaluations in the class. It also says that his disability affects his writing speed and his communication skills and that he learns most effectively when information is visual. This gives the instructor basic but helpful information about Eric's learning style and how best to help him be successful in the class.

The letter to instructors also lists the accommodations the student qualifies for. It includes a description of the responsibilities of the instructor, the student, and the DSS office in providing each of the accommodations. It also asks the instructor to make an announcement at the beginning of the semester inviting all students with disabilities to schedule an appointment with the instructor to discuss the course and the accommodations that will be needed. As part of the student's responsibilities it states that the instructor is under no obligation to implement accommodations if the student does not meet with the instructor.

Here is another example of the importance of students being able to advocate for themselves. Depending on the accommodation requested, the student will need to meet with the instructor at least once at the beginning of the course to talk about the accommodations. Whenever possible my son prefers to hand the instructor the forms that need to be signed rather than sitting down and discussing his own particular needs. It is always better if the student is able to have a dialogue with the instructor about their possible needs in the class. More will be discussed in Chapter 7 about the issues related to disclosing more information about the disability or the learning style of the student.

One of the most important accommodations that Eric receives is a single dormitory room. He lives in a smaller room for just one student with no roommate. Many colleges will offer this as an option for students. When researching whether the college offers this option, make sure you talk to someone who knows the school's policy on this. When I called Eric's university housing office I spoke to an individual who said only students with medical issues such as allergies and asthma can qualify for a single room. I pursued this further and found someone at the same office who informed me that students can have single rooms for other reasons. The college will probably require documentation about the disability and the student's reasons for needing a single room. The documentation should emphasize the social difficulties for students on the autism spectrum as well as the sensory issues that would make living with another person difficult for a student on the autism spectrum.

The single room is more expensive than a room with a roommate but it has been worth the cost. Eric needs his own space and needs to be able to close his door and be alone and not have to socialize with anyone if he doesn't want to. Studying is easier for him without distractions from a roommate. The social component of living with someone would have been stressful for Eric. I don't believe that living in a single room has been isolating for Eric because his room is part of a suite of rooms and there are ample opportunities for socializing with other students. Eric doesn't seem to stand out as being different because there are quite a few single rooms in the dormitories on campus and many students choose to live alone for different reasons. The choice of a single room or not should be made by the student and based on his or her individual needs.

Besides having a single room, there aren't many accommodations available to help the student deal with the noises and social situations of living in a dormitory. The student will need to be as prepared as possible for what that environment is like. A visit to a dorm beforehand can help prepare the student. If the parents went to college themselves they can try to describe what the experience was like for them. If sensory issues are a problem the student may need some strategies for dealing with those issues. The sensory experience of living in close proximity to so many people is a challenge for many new students in college.

Students have to learn to respect or tolerate the individual differences and lifestyles that may surround them in a dorm setting. The student may be bothered by the choices that other students around them make. If there are problems or students have a complaint, they have to know whom to go to and how to advocate for themselves. Some students adjust well to having a roommate and living in a dormitory but the majority of students who have an autism spectrum diagnosis have difficulties adjusting to dormitory life. Some students may prefer to live off-campus in an apartment where they can be more independent and not be bothered by the noise and social expectations of dormitory life. One adult on the spectrum once told me that living in his own apartment was helpful to him because it provided a safe "home base" to operate from. He felt more comfortable socializing when he knew he had a quiet place to return to afterwards.

In addition to the single room, my son receives accommodations that have benefited him academically. A seemingly simple accommodation of priority registration allows Eric to register for his next semester's courses before other students. Courses can fill up very quickly in college, especially those courses that are popular or meet general education requirements. At times Eric has had to retake certain courses before taking others and without this accommodation he would have had difficulty getting into the courses he needed. Priority registration also allows the student more choices of class times. For example, if the student does not do well in the early morning, priority registration gives them more choices of classes later in the day. It also can be helpful for students on the autism spectrum to schedule their courses so that they have more time between classes and don't have to hurry to get from one class to another. Priority registration can give the student more courses to choose from to arrange the best schedule for that particular student.

Some colleges or universities may consider a student's request to waive certain required courses. For example, foreign languages can sometimes be challenging for students on the autism spectrum. The school may waive this requirement if the request is supported by documentation from the office of Disabilities Services. By no means is it the norm for colleges to allow students to waive required courses and students and their parents should not count on this option. If a student must take a particular course in college that they know will be especially difficult, they can consider taking just that course during a summer session when they can concentrate fully on the academic work for that one course. Another option is for the student to take the course with a pass/fail option where they would only need to pass the course and would not risk lowering their grade point average if they did not do well.

During the first two years of college Eric took 12 hours per week of courses each semester, which is the minimum required to be a full-time student. (A student must be considered a full-time student to live in residential housing on campus.) This lower course load reduced the academic stress on Eric as he adjusted to the college environment and his new responsibilities. It can be a good option to consider for a student on the autism spectrum. I discovered at orientation that it is no longer typical for students to graduate from college in four years as it was when I was a college student. Most students these days, with or without disabilities, need at least five years to complete a degree and many students need more than that. If it is not too much of a financial burden to take college more slowly and allow the student to take a smaller course load, it could improve the student's overall stress level. It can also give the student time to build up their study skills as they adjust to the rigors of college academics.

A student should investigate specific classes before they register for them. Starting well before the time to register, the student can ask questions about the courses and the instructors. They can talk to other students, their academic advisor, or the instructor of the particular class being considered. The student can sometimes find the course syllabus online and the objectives, textbook, and readings that are required for the course. The student can also audit a class. In this situation the student can observe the class for a limited period of time to determine whether it is an appropriate class for them.

Many colleges will offer introduction or orientation courses for new students. At Eric's university an orientation course is required for freshmen students for each individual college within the university. Orientation courses often provide instruction on how to use the library and other school facilities, how to register for courses, and how to explore career options for a particular major. They may also include part of the curriculum on developing better study skills.

Priority seating is another accommodation that is available and can be beneficial to a student on the autism spectrum. Sitting in the front of the classroom closer to the instructor may help the student hear the instructor and follow notes written on the blackboard. It may also cut down on distractions for the student. Eric has had several instructors from other countries with strong accents that at times made it difficult for him to understand them. Sitting in the front of the classroom helped. In very large classes it may be important for the student to sit at the end of a row where only one student is next to them or sit near the door to the classroom for easy exiting. The student will need to discuss his or her seating needs with the professor at the beginning of the course. If the student receives this accommodation and seating is assigned in the class, the student should be allowed to pick the seat that best meets their needs. It may be important for the student to arrive to classes early, especially during the first week of classes, so that they can pick out where they want to sit before the other students arrive.

Some students with an autism spectrum diagnosis have fine motor difficulties that make handwriting difficult or slower. They may write too slowly or their handwriting may be messy. Some students may be perfectionists about having the words and letters look just right. Others may only be comfortable taking notes in complete sentences during lectures. This can definitely slow down their note taking in class. Some students with writing difficulties may choose to type their notes on a laptop computer during lectures. This is allowed in most college classrooms.

Eric received occupational therapy throughout public school for fine motor delays and motor planning issues. Handwriting notes during a college lecture can be difficult for him. He also occasionally has trouble knowing what the main points that he should write down are in the lecture. He receives an accommodation in college for a scribe or note taker in classes when he needs it. In most classes the instructor will make an announcement at the beginning of the course that note takers are needed and will ask for volunteers. The volunteer student scribes can go to the DSS website for instructions about how to organize their notes, what information to include, and the importance of their responsibility as note takers for other students. Students volunteering to supply this service also receive a notebook of special paper that automatically makes copies of what is written. Eric's responsibility for getting this accommodation is to approach the student volunteering to be a scribe, introduce himself, and make arrangements for getting copies of that student's notes. If possible the student getting the accommodation should be encouraged to also take notes during class as best they can. They will benefit from practicing taking notes and can then use the copies of another student's notes to supplement their own.

Tape recording lectures is another accommodation available at colleges that can help students who have difficulty keeping up with note taking. The student must arrange this accommodation with the instructor. The student signs an agreement that states that they will not release, copy, or allow anyone else to use the tapes. The tapes are returned to the instructor at the conclusion of the semester. Tape recording lectures allows the student to listen to the taped lecture to get any information they might have missed during class. This can be helpful for the student who is easily distracted during a class or has trouble focusing on what the instructor is saying. The student can listen to the recording later in a quiet setting when they are better able to focus.

Students with learning disabilities as well as students on the autism spectrum may benefit from extended time on testing. This is a very commonly used accommodation in college and many instructors are going to have experience with this accommodation for students. There is paperwork that has to be completed between the DSS office, the student, and the instructor. A time must be scheduled by the student to take the test either at the department or at another location, usually the DSS office. A distraction-free room can be arranged at the DSS office if needed. The instructor must get a copy of the test to the DSS office by the scheduled time of testing. Instructors can choose to have the student deliver the test in a sealed and signed envelope, fax or e-mail the test directly to the DSS office, or hand deliver it themselves. Similar options are available for the student to return the test to the instructor.

Some instructors require students using this accommodation to take the test during the same time the other students in the class are taking the test. Some may be more flexible and allow the student to schedule the test at another time the same day. If there is flexibility in scheduling exam times, students may want to space out their exams carefully to allow appropriate time between each exam for studying. At the testing site, the time students are allowed to work on the test is monitored carefully so that they get the required time. Students are allowed up to double the time the rest of the class is given to complete a test or exam.

The week of exams is a stressful time for all students in college. Exams weigh heavily toward the final grade a student will receive for a course. The student may be anxious about passing or failing a class or they may be overwhelmed by the amount of material they need to review for the exam. Some students may have difficulty prioritizing which courses to study for first and how to divide their studying time between each course. Some instructors will give students advanced preparation for an exam by providing practice tests, giving students a written list of what material will be covered on the exam, and by offering review sessions for the students. If the instructor does not do these things, the student can always ask the instructor for more information about the upcoming exam. The student can ask the instructor what kind of exam it will be—essay, multiple choice, short answer, etc. This information will give the student a better idea of how to prepare. The student can also ask an instructor what they think are the most important areas to review to prepare for the exam. Most instructors will not mind giving students guidance on this if they are asked.

Most colleges are going to offer tutoring services for students. It is typically available for all students, not just students with learning disabilities. At Eric's university the tutoring is free for most beginning-level courses. Students must first schedule and attend an orientation each semester in order to apply for tutoring by appointment. Once their application is processed, the students can receive tutoring in up to two subjects for a maximum of two hours per week in each of the subjects. Some students want weekly tutoring sessions whereas others may only need an occasional tutoring session. There are drop-in tutoring sessions available for those students who need more immediate help with a concept or problem. No appointment is necessary for these sessions and the hours of drop in are typically posted on the internet or at the tutoring office. Keep in mind that for drop-in tutoring sessions the student needing assistance will most likely be assigned a different tutor each time they come in for help. The amount of time a student will receive tutoring services will depend on their need and will be evaluated by the tutor. As the student progresses to more advanced courses in their major, they may have more difficulty finding tutoring help.

There are other opportunities for students to receive help with the academics at college. Some instructors hold study groups for their courses and review sessions before tests. Some instructors will schedule study group sessions for the students to get together and study without the instructor present. Frequently instructors will put study guides on their website for students to use before a test. This is a wonderful resource for those students who may have difficulty determining the most important information to study for a test. Many of the instructors at Eric's school post lecture notes on the website as well. A student can print out the lecture notes before going to a class, take the notes with them, and use them to help follow along with that day's lecture. This is very helpful to students who are visual learners. It is also helpful if a student is ill and can't attend class. Some instructors' websites may also include upcoming assignments and test dates as well as test grades. I am constantly amazed at the benefits of the computer technology available to students today.

Despite all the new technology and the tutors or study groups available, a student at one time or another will most likely have to communicate with the instructor about an assignment or about the course. Instructors are required to have regular office hours in which to meet with students. These hours are usually posted at the instructor's office, listed on their website, and are written on the syllabus the student receives during the first week of class. However, most communication between students and instructors is done by e-mail. If the student needs to talk to the professor in person, they can arrange an appointment through e-mail.

Students are also encouraged to write to the instructor with questions about assignments and projects. If a student has a family emergency or is sick they can let the instructor know by e-mail and get assignments they miss.

A student may have difficulty when they must meet with an instructor in person. Initiating conversations can be hard for many students who have an autism spectrum disorder. One strategy could be for the student to write down ahead of time a list of things they need to talk to the instructor about or a list of questions. Another strategy might be to contact the instructor ahead of time by e-mail, letting them know what the student will need to talk about during their upcoming meeting. The student could also prepare for a meeting with an instructor by role playing with a parent or the service provider from DSS to practice what he or she wants to say beforehand. The more prepared the student is before the meeting, the more comfortable the student will be, and the better the meeting will go. Some colleges will have service providers available to attend meetings with the student if requested.

In smaller college settings students often find it easier to get to know instructors. The student may take multiple classes from the same instructor over the course of their college career. The student learns that particular instructor's teaching style and can possibly develop a personal relationship where they feel more comfortable talking about their learning strengths and challenges. No matter what size the college or university, if an instructor is particularly supportive or understanding the student should try to take as many courses with that instructor as possible.

Students may need to ask instructors for individual accommodations within a particular class in addition to the accommodations they receive from disabilities services. One example might be the student asking to do computer-lab work from home rather than having a lab partner. Some students may have difficulty working in a computer lab full of people. Students may want to request working individually rather than in groups on projects. Or a student may inform an instructor that they may need to occasionally walk out during a class if they are getting overwhelmed. All of these examples reflect an individual student's needs and whether they are allowed is up to each instructor. A student should feel free to talk to the instructor about any problems they are having in the class.

One person whom all students have to meet with during their college career is their academic advisor. This person is usually a professor within the department of the student's major. The department assigns an advisor to each student at the time the student declares their major. This person normally remains the student's advisor throughout their time in college unless there is a change in the course of study or the professor leaves the college.

The role of the academic advisor is to assist the student in planning their academic program. They give the student information about the courses needed for graduation and make sure the student is staying on track with the required curriculum. The student must meet with their academic advisor before registering for courses each semester. The advisor will check the student's proposed course selection and advise them about any changes they should make to improve their academic path. A student will also need to consult with their academic advisor when dropping a class or adding a class. A good relationship between the student and their advisor can be very helpful for the student on the autism spectrum who may need guidance in this area. Unless the student self-discloses to the academic advisor about his or her disability, the advisor will only know that the student is receiving support from Disabilities Services. Students may want to consider explaining more about their disability to their academic advisor if they will be taking fewer courses each semester or if they will need more guidance on career choices.

Even with the guidance of an academic advisor, students will most likely need additional guidance from parents about academic choices. The advisor is experienced in the curriculum of the student's major, but they are not experienced in autism nor will they understand the student's individual needs and learning style. Parents can be a good resource for the student in deciding what courses to take, how to balance difficult and easier courses, and the amount of hours the student should take.

The student on the autism spectrum will probably have more contact with the Disabilities Services office than any other office on campus. It helps for the student to develop a comfort level with the DSS office, not only with their service provider but also with the staff who greet them and help them schedule appointments or testing dates. One way to do this is to have regular scheduled appointments with the service provider.

How often the student meets with the service provider will depend on the case load and schedule of the provider as well as the needs of the student. Eric meets with his service provider once a week at a set day and time. This way the appointment is easier for Eric to remember. At some meetings there are important items to discuss and sometimes the appointment is mainly a "checking in" to make sure everything is going well.

The service provider can be the most important resource for the student with a disability in college. This person will be assigned to the student when they first enter the school and should remain their contact person throughout their years in college. A good relationship between the student and the service provider is critical. This is the person the student should feel comfortable with and trust enough to come to if they need help or are in trouble. This person also needs to understand the student as an individual, to know what is hard for them and to understand their learning style. Understanding the student's needs is not something that happens overnight. The documentation submitted to DSS about the student's disability describes some of the issues the student may have but may not adequately explain the strengths and the weaknesses of the individual student that can only be learned over time. Spending time with the student is the best way to understand where their difficulties may lie, especially in the areas of communication skills and social skills. Time spent with the student will give the service provider good information about that student's self-advocacy skills and where he or she may need some extra help to improve these skills.

Parents can help support the relationship between the student and the service provider in several ways. They can make sure the provider has current and accurate information about the student in the documentation given to the Disabilities Services office. Parents can also support this relationship by being knowledgeable about the laws that protect the student with a disability in college. Once they understand the legal differences from high school, parents can better understand the role of the service provider and their own changing role as a parent. Parents must allow the staff from Disabilities Services to work with the student under the legal guidelines they are required to adhere to. Last, but probably most important, the parents can support this relationship by encouraging the student to reach out to the service provider on a regular basis and whenever they need help or someone to talk to.

As mentioned before, many students on the autism spectrum may have difficulties initiating conversations and explaining to others about problems they may be having. Sometimes my son will be having difficulties in a particular class but not understand he is having a problem or how serious the problem is until it is too late. Eric has made poor final grades in classes where he thought he was doing fine. If Eric does realize he needs help in a class, he may have difficulty asking for that help. He may not know exactly what the problem is or why he is making poor grades and so he won't know what specific help to ask for. This is where the DSS service provider can really help. The service provider needs to ask Eric the right questions to help him share information about the problem. They can then problem solve together to determine strategies that can help.

Asking the right questions is crucial for the service provider to be able to help the student on the autism spectrum. A general, "How are things going?" kind of question will not typically get much of a response from a student. The student may answer, "Fine" or "OK" and not elaborate on details about the class. If the service provider really wants to know about a student's progress in a course, they must ask more specific questions about the course or about the assignments. Questions about a particular paper or test will often produce more useful information from the student and possibly a better understanding of how the student is doing in the class or whether they understand the material. If the student has difficulty seeing that they may be having a problem in a particular class, the service provider can ask questions about the requirements of the course or the current grades the student is making in the class. Their doing this can help the student understand if they are not meeting the expectations of the class. After getting to know the student, the service provider should know what is difficult for the student and will know what kinds of questions to ask.

Eric's relationship with his service provider has become very important to him. He feels comfortable with her and knows that he can go to her with any questions or problems he may have at college. Sometimes she is the person who can help him directly with his problem and sometimes she gives him the name and contact number for someone else on campus who is a more appropriate resource. She has become a case manager of sorts, directing Eric to other services on campus as he needs them. In addition to the help with scheduling courses and accessing accommodations for his courses, she keeps him on track in many ways. She may remind him about upcoming deadlines or help him with organizational strategies. She helps him problem solve or make decisions. She never tells him what to do but instead helps him understand a problem and analyze his choices.

After Eric has met with his service provider to address a particular problem or issue, she will frequently send Eric an e-mail summarizing what was discussed at their meeting. She may list the things that were discussed or the steps they took together to work on an issue. The service provider also includes in the e-mail a reminder of the next steps Eric needs to take and a timeline if needed. Having a written summary of the meeting helps Eric by clarifying his progress on a particular problem.

Any college student may experience academic stresses. The DSS service provider can be a resource for the student in determining strategies to help with these stresses. The stresses can include issues such as dealing with an instructor who isn't flexible with assignments or timelines, coping in a course that may be going too fast for the student to keep up, or making up coursework if the student has to miss some classes. The service provider can problem solve with the student to help them deal with situations such as these. If more counseling would be beneficial, the service provider can refer the student to the counseling office on campus.

Most colleges offer counseling services to students experiencing academic or personal problems. All students in college, not just students with disabilities, can find themselves overwhelmed, depressed, or anxious and may need to speak to someone. Most counseling centers have regular office hours when students can make appointments to speak to a counselor. They also typically have after-hours on-call counselors available for students. Confidentiality is assured and many of the services from the counseling office are free to students enrolled in the university. Counseling services are primarily short term but referrals can be made to long-term supports and resources in the community if needed. Many counseling offices also offer workshops to students on such topics as dealing with stress, study skills, body image and eating issues, depression, relaxation techniques, etc. If the student needs individual support, they will probably need to disclose to the counselor the nature of their disability in order for the support to be helpful. Some students may choose to receive counseling from a psychologist or physician in the community whom they know and who is already aware of the student's needs.

What do parents do when their son or daughter does not want to use the accommodations or services offered by the college? Unfortunately there is not much a parent can do in this situation. Legally the decision to pursue accommodations or services and use them is totally up to the students if they are over 18 and are their own guardians. There can be many reasons why a student decides not to use an accommodation. Some students may be uncomfortable receiving any kind of support in a class that may bring attention to them or make them feel different from the other students. The student might benefit from having a note taker in a class, but find it too difficult to communicate with another student to set up this accommodation. Students also may not think they need the accommodation because they believe they can do the work successfully without any support. If the student decides not to use accommodations, the parents need to communicate with the student frequently to keep apprised of how they are doing. The parents can be available to offer support to the student if needed and remind them of the services they can access through the college. Unfortunately, it may be after the student goes through a difficult experience or fails academically that they realize their need for help.

There have been other fairly simple strategies that have helped my son academically in college. One is a calendar he uses in his dorm room. It is a large calendar of the sort that people often place on the top of a desk. Eric uses it to keep track of all of his meetings with his service provider and his academic advisor. He also uses it to remind himself of upcoming tests, projects, and papers. When Eric gets the syllabus for a course during the first week of class, he records all the important dates on the syllabus onto his calendar in his room. He has learned that it is also helpful to include notes on the calendar about when to start working on the different steps of a paper or project. The calendar is placed right above his desk where he does his school work so he can see it. It helps Eric to have a visible reminder of the whole month ahead. He also uses a smaller assignment notebook/calendar to record assignments that are given in class.

Some students may have difficulty keeping track of their grades and overall progress in a course. As I mentioned earlier, Eric has been surprised a few times when he got poor final grades in a class. One solution that has helped him is to record all the grades he receives in a notebook. The service provider helped Eric develop a routine of recording grades in this notebook as soon as he gets them. He brings the notebook with him to his meeting with the service provider and she can go over the grades with him. The act of checking the grades helps initiate conversations about how Eric is doing in each class and whether he understands the material.

Eric has learned to make rules to help him stay more organized and keep up with his coursework. He once had an instructor complain that he never picked up tests after they have been graded. Eric made a rule to always pick up graded tests from a class and use them to study for the final exam. In courses required for his major where his grades are very important, Eric made a rule always to do any extra credit work if it is available in these courses. Recording upcoming test and project dates from the syllabus onto his calendar is another rule that he developed because of problems in this area. Some students may need rules written down where they can see them and be reminded of them. Some students, like Eric, can keep track of them in their heads. As the student learns the areas where they need to improve, they can apply rules to help them be more successful.

Frequently, students have trouble knowing when to ask for help in a course. One strategy is to write a guideline or a list of rules for asking for help. This could be created with the service provider's help or the parents' help. The guideline would designate set times the student should initiate asking for help from an instructor. These could include such situations as when the student fails a pop quiz, or when they have two unmet deadlines in a row. Other examples could be when the student doesn't understand a homework assignment or when they get two grade Cs in a row on graded assignments. The student and service provider together could decide what criteria would be appropriate for each class. It can also be helpful if there are set times during a semester when the student communicates with each instructor and discusses his or her progress in each class.

College instructors are being challenged with a growing number of learning needs for their students. They are becoming accustomed to teaching students who are receiving accommodations through Disabilities Services on campus. Many Disabilities Services offices will provide faculty workshops to educate instructors about the laws protecting students with disabilities and general strategies for helping students. Sometimes information sheets about a particular disability can be sent to instructors with the accommodations letter if requested by the student. In addition to accommodations, instructors can implement strategies themselves that can make things easier for students on the autism spectrum. Many of these teaching strategies can also benefit students without disabilities.

The Montgomery College Disability Support Services office suggests some strategies that instructors have found to be helpful for students with disabilities. During the registration process the instructor can have the syllabus for the course available early for students. All expectations for the course should be included in the syllabus and be very clear to the student. They can also have a list of textbooks or readings available so the student can begin reading early for the course. The student would also benefit from the instructor choosing a textbook that has a study guide included.

In addition to strategies during the registration process, an instructor can use strategies during instruction of the course to help students with disabilities. Because many students may have difficulty approaching an instructor about accommodations, the instructor may need to make his or her willingness to work with students with disabilities known. They can include a statement in the syllabus or make an announcement in class about how students can contact them about accommodations. Instructors can summarize important points from the previous class at the beginning of each class and highlight the important points made at the end of every class. Students who are visual learners will also benefit from the instructor using visual aids during a lecture. The instructor can break down long-range writing assignments into steps with due dates for each part of the assignment. This allows the student to get continuous feedback from the instructor while working on the assignment. Instructors can provide study help to students by helping develop study groups for the class and by providing study questions and review sessions before exams. These strategies are fairly easy to provide and could make a big difference in the success of students with disabilities. They could also benefit all the students in the class, including the student on the autism spectrum (Montgomery College Disability Support Services 2004).

Other simple teaching strategies can be used that would be helpful to students on the autism spectrum. The instructor should give advance notice about any changes in course requirements, assignment due dates, or tests. The instructor's expectations should be direct and they should not expect students automatically to be able to generalize instructions from one assignment to another. In lectures, instructors can avoid idioms and sarcasm unless they also explain them. They can present new vocabulary on the blackboard or use a student handout. They can also provide opportunities for questions and answers during a lecture. Also, if the student must work in small groups or with a partner in the class, the instructor should consider giving individual assignments to each student. The student on the autism spectrum may have difficulty with the social components required to work in a group or with a partner.

One of the most difficult areas for any student in college is the social arena. Many adults on the spectrum who speak about their college experiences describe the difficulties involved in being accepted and making friends on a college campus. Interpersonal relationships can be very challenging for a student on the autism spectrum. Unfortunately, supports for developing a social network are frequently not available for students on the autism spectrum in college. The counseling office provides a place students can go to discuss their concerns but there are often no supports in place to deal with helping the student make friends and be involved socially on campus. Some colleges may have a peer helper program available for students, but most universities and colleges do not offer this service. The DSS service provider may be able to offer the student some guidance in this area but they are typically not equipped to address this issue and do not have the time to do so.

Most colleges have various student organizations and clubs that can be possible social outlets for students. At large universities there may be hundreds of organizations for students. At Eric's school there are over

200 student organizations including groups connected with the arts, sports, government, political action, religion, ethnic diversity, etc. A student may be able to find a club on campus that involves a favorite interest such as chess, badminton, bowling, or accounting. There are service organizations as well where students can participate in community service or volunteer opportunities. If the student expresses an interest in social opportunities, parents may want to encourage the student to research what organizations are available at their college.

It is helpful if the student sets some goals for what they want to gain from joining a club or organization. Maybe they want to find friends, get some exercise, or just have fun. Maybe they want career opportunities or want to broaden their interests. They should think about why they want to join and ask themselves if that particular organization fits their needs. Students will need to consider whether the other members have similar interests and values, if there are any dues required, and how much of a commitment they would have to make to the organization.

I was recently contacted by a student at my son's university who, along with other members of a scholars program on campus, wanted to develop a peer support program that would be available for students on the autism spectrum at the university. A volunteer peer would get together socially with the student on the autism spectrum to go out to eat, or go to a movie or an event on campus, or do something that the student chose to do. A program like this could be very helpful to those students who want more social outlets but struggle to participate in college activities. This volunteer program is a good example of how the social support piece of the college experience can be developed with some motivated individuals and creative thinking.

Many students on the autism spectrum have problems in college that are not academic related but related more to self-help, time management, interpersonal skills, or organizational skills. The supports available on campus for students with disabilities may not be able to address these issues. Parents can be supportive, but they may not be nearby or the student may prefer this support from a non-family member. Some colleges may offer a study consultant, usually an upperclassman, who is available to meet with the student and help with organizational issues related to assignments and testing. This is not offered by all colleges so a student should ask the school whether a service like this is available.

If the student needs this service and it is not available through the school there may be coaching services available from private agencies or psychologists in private practice in the community. These coaches would have regular contact with the student to help them stay organized and to talk about any problems that may come up on a day-to-day basis. The student may find a coach who has personal experience with working with individuals on the autism spectrum. Some students may have friends or individuals in their lives who would be willing to contact them regularly and oversee how they are doing. Families may need to be creative to find what helps.

The state Vocational Rehabilitation (VR) Services Program may also be a resource for students in college. States receive federal grants to operate VR programs. In addition to financial support, VR can offer vocational counseling and guidance, vocational training, transportation when appropriate, and services to assist students in transitioning from school to work. To be eligible for services, a student must have a disability that results in a "substantial impediment to employment." The individual must also show that he or she can benefit from VR services to achieve employment (State VR Services Program Fact Sheet 2003, p.1).

Once a student is judged to qualify for VR services, they are assigned a VR counselor. That individual gathers information about the student's work history, education, and training. The VR counselor also looks at the student's abilities, interests, and goals for the future. An Individualized Plan for Employment (IPE) is developed by the student alone or with the assistance of the VR counselor and anyone else interested in helping the student. It should list the steps necessary for the student to achieve employment, the services the student may need, and how progress is going to be evaluated towards the student's goals. The services determined to be needed by the student may be provided by the VR counselor or by other providers in the community.

Depending on the student's financial resources, the State VR agency may require payment for some services. As I mentioned in Chapter 3, if the student is receiving Social Security Income (SSI) they automatically qualify for financial assistance. There are also VR services that are available to all eligible individuals without charge. They include assessments to determine VR needs, vocational counseling and guidance, and job search and placement services. Information about the VR agency in your state is generally listed under "State Government" in the telephone directory. There is also a website listed under Rehabilitative Services Administration in Appendix A.

In addition to the supports provided by the college and supports from outside agencies or individuals, the parents are an important part of the support system for the student in college. The student must now advocate for themselves but the parents can still play an integral part in the success of the student in college. Parents don't attend meetings anymore or make decisions for the student, but they can and should remain involved in the student's life. If the parents are not located near the student's school they can still stay involved. Communication, by e-mail or by phone, may need to occur frequently between the parents and the student if the student needs the parents' support. Donna Kruger, a parent of a son in college, describes the role of the parent as "an advocate to keep the path as clear and smooth as possible when the going gets rough and to provide lots of support and encouragement" (Kruger 2001, p.19).

In the earlier years of school parents are encouraged and expected to participate in their child's educational life. The role of the parent changes, however, when the student with a disability graduates from high school. From this point on the parents provide support more as a mentor or advisor. It is not an easy adjustment and resources are hard to find to help parents with this new phase of parenting. The challenge for parents is to know how to be supportive to the student and still encourage their independence.

No matter how much we trust them to do the right thing, it is hard for parents to let their children learn from their mistakes, especially when the consequences of their mistakes can be serious. Every parent worries about their child making bad decisions and being in dangerous situations. That worry is most likely magnified for parents of students on the autism spectrum. If the parent is lucky enough to have a student who tells them about their life at school, they must learn to distinguish between the everyday problems the student may report and the more serious situations. Good communication between the parents and the student is crucial. Situations that threaten the student's safety or health, depression, serious financial problems—all can necessitate a parent being more actively involved with the student's life. A parent should provide resources and information and support directly to the student first. Helping the student gather information and understand their options may be enough. If more is necessary, the parent may need to contact the Disability Services office to report their concerns.

One of the ways I support Eric at college is in helping him during the registration process each semester. I help him with the organizational part of the registration process. Sometimes I print out a list of the courses he still needs for his major and what required courses he has already taken. We check the prerequisites for the required courses to make sure he qualifies to take them. I also can help Eric go online to see which of the needed courses are offered that coming semester and make a list of possible times they are available. It can be very complicated to process all this information and then to fit everything into a schedule that is balanced and works for the student. Eric always makes the decisions about which courses he wants to take but it helps him to have some of the background work done beforehand. We always gather the information together and, as he has gotten more familiar with this process, he has been able to do more and more of it himself.

I also sometimes advise Eric about the combination of courses to take during a semester. I remind him to select classes that are better suited to his strengths and interests and to balance these with the required courses that are harder. Some students on the autism spectrum do better in courses that are focused more on concrete information, courses that require more memorization skills. Philosophy courses, for example, may be too abstract and more difficult for some students. Without some guidance in course selection students can end up with a schedule that is too difficult.

If Eric needs information or help from someone on campus, his academic advisor or DSS service provider or another person on campus, I sometimes help him prepare for these meetings. We talk about exactly what information he needs and how he can ask for it. I may give him suggestions of possible questions he might want to ask. I may also talk to him about what information the person may need from him and remind him of any documents or information he should take with him to the meeting. He will frequently write down what information he will need to get from this meeting as a reminder for himself. Eric seems to appreciate this help and it makes it less stressful for him if he has some guidance and preparation beforehand.

Another way parents can help their son or daughter in college is with reminders. If you stay involved enough you can know about upcoming deadlines or procedures that all students must deal with such as registering for classes, signing up for meal plans or for dorm rooms. I often remind Eric the week before he has to do something that the date is coming up. He will write it in his calendar and have a better chance of remembering it. With countless things to keep track of, a student can benefit from an occasional reminder of events coming up.

One of the basic ways parents can support students on the autism spectrum at college is by helping them feel confident about themselves and proud of what they have accomplished. We know college can be stressful, and encouraging the student and complimenting their efforts is important in helping them feel good about themselves. Other students may have ways to ask for reassurance or praise from parents. The student who has an autism spectrum disorder may not do that, so parents may need to remind the student how proud they are of them and do it frequently.

I don't really know what goes on with Eric on a day-to-day basis while he is at school. I have to rely on him to share the important information with me about how he is doing. I can ask the right questions, but if he doesn't want to tell me information I can't do anything about it. Before Eric went to college we talked about the need for me to stay involved in certain areas while he is at college. I emphasized that I would respect his privacy and would not expect him to tell me about his personal life, but that I would like to ask questions and get updates on how he is doing in his classes. Eric understands enough about his disability for him to know he may need some extra help at times and he is comfortable with having my help. If parents are fortunate enough to have a son or daughter who is open to their help, they need to remember to not misuse that trust. Parents have to give the student freedom to make their own personal decisions—and sometimes to make mistakes.

7 Self-Awareness and the Issue of Self-Disclosure

Success in college can be significantly affected by how students on the autism spectrum feel about themselves and their understanding and acceptance of their strengths and differences. College life can be stressful for any student. Dealing with that stress can be easier if the student has good self-esteem and self-awareness. For students with a disability, understanding and accepting the diagnosis will help them be stronger advocates for the supports they may need in college.

Self-determination has become a popular phrase in the literature on disabilities. Self-determination was defined by Martin and Huber Marshall as consisting of seven important components:

- *Self-awareness*—the ability to identify and understand one's needs and strengths.

- *Self-advocacy*—the ability to express those needs and strengths.

- *Self-efficacy or self-confidence*—the belief that one will reach a goal.

- *Decision-making*—the set of skills needed to choose the best option to reach one's goals.

- *Independent performance*—the ability to start and complete tasks independently.

- *Self-evaluation*—the ability to assess one's performance and know when a goal has been reached.

- *Adjustment*—revising one's goals to improve success.

(NCSET 2004, p.1).

The result of successful self-determination is that students learn to take control over the things that are critical to their life. Nowhere is this more important than in college, where students are often faced for the first time with making important decisions and advocating for themselves. After high school graduation, students with disabilities are no longer entitled to the same services and must disclose and sometimes defend their need for accommodations to the Disabilities Services office on campus. They may also have to describe their needs to instructors or to other students. According to the above definition of self-determination, the student must understand their disability, must be able to express their needs, must believe in themselves, and must be able to make decisions independently and complete the tasks needed to reach their goals. This may seem like an impossible challenge for some students on the autism spectrum.

There are different ways that parents can help the student learn these important skills before they transition to college. Parents can begin building the student's self-awareness at the time they first learn about their differences. No matter what the age of the student when they learn of their diagnosis, the information that is given them should be honest, positive, and easy to understand. The information should be individualized for the student so that it describes that student's strengths, weaknesses, and how the autism or Asperger Syndrome affects their day-to-day lives. The student will develop better self-advocacy skills if they understand why some things may be harder for them and how they can ask for help if needed.

Another way parents can help students learn self-determination skills is to allow them to make decisions in their lives even if the results are not always positive. Parents may find it easier to make the decisions for the student or may feel that the student is not capable of making certain decisions in their lives. Often parents may make decisions for the student because they are afraid of the student failing or being hurt or rejected. Important decisions related to the student's safety or health may not be the appropriate ones to let the student practice making independently. But there are many other opportunities where the student can be involved in voicing desires and opinions and making their own choices. Although it is hard for parents to let their children make mistakes, it is important to allow them the opportunities to learn from their mistakes.

One decision students can make in their own lives is whether to get involved in the autism community. Participation in the autism community may provide an opportunity to connect with other individuals on the autism spectrum and their families. It can give the student experience in advocating and sharing information about the autism spectrum with the community. Students can develop better self-awareness as they learn more about the spectrum and how their own strengths and weaknesses may be shared by others. Just as parents of newly diagnosed children may want to reach out to others in a similar position, students on the spectrum may feel less alone when they are able to meet or talk to other individuals who know what they are going through. It may be extremely helpful to a student to feel they are a part of a group that accepts them for who they are and where explanations for behaviors are not necessary. There are often support groups in local communities as well as national organizations students can join. Students can also explore the websites that are available for individuals on the autism spectrum.

Students can also develop their self-determination skills through becoming involved whenever possible in school decisions and IEP meetings. Students can make their wishes and needs known and practice communicating and problem solving. This is critical in the student's later years of high school when they are approaching the transition to college, but involvement in school decisions and meetings can be started much earlier. The student may not be able to participate actively in school decisions when they are very young. However, they can understand why they might need help at school, that other students need help at times too, and that there are people at school who are there to help them. Knowing this information helps build on their self-awareness and ultimately their ability to advocate for themselves in the future.

Parents who are aware of just how important self-advocacy skills are going to be for the adult student can better prepare the student to use them in college. Many parents do not realize how their advocacy role changes for a student with a disability when he or she is an adult. Many of the things parents have done for the student in the past are now going to be the student's responsibility. I always thought that I was fairly knowledgeable about autism and the supports and services in school, but I was surprised by the degree of self-advocacy needed by students with disabilities in college. Many parents may not realize how important self-advocacy is until they begin preparing themselves for the student's transition to college. Preparing the student to be a strong self-advocate can and should be started much earlier.

Schools can help educate students and their parents about the need for self-awareness and self-advocacy in college. Unfortunately, schools don't always address these issues early enough. The rights of adults with disabilities and the need for good self-advocacy skills may not be addressed until the student's Transition Plan meeting. Schools must invite a student with a disability to attend IEP meetings, but they don't typically encourage them to attend. Parents should encourage the student to participate in meetings in whatever manner is most appropriate for the student. (More information about creative ways to include a student on the autism spectrum in meetings is covered in Chapter 2.) Parents should also initiate or recommend goals for the IEP in the area of self-advocacy.

The college student's choice to self-disclose must be their decision, and only their decision. Parents can talk to the student and share with them their opinions about self-disclosure but the decision is ultimately the student's. My son's experience with disclosing has been positive and has definitely made a difference in his success at college. Eric has been comfortable sharing information about himself with people who have needed to know. Not all students will feel this way, however, and parents need to respect whatever decision the student makes about self-disclosure.

The accommodations that colleges provide can make the difference between academic success and failure for many students. Some students do fine without academic accommodations and may not feel the need to disclose to Disabilities Services for academic supports. Even if the student doesn't require accommodations in the classroom, they may require other individuals on campus to understand their needs related to their disability. Student health services, the counseling center, housing services, and career counseling all offer services that may help the student. If the student needs special considerations from these offices because of their disability, documentation on record with Disabilities Services can help support any special requests or services.

The confidentiality issue surrounding disclosure about a disability may be a concern for some students. The Family Educational Rights and Privacy Act of 1974 (FERPA), P.L. 93–380, protects the confidentiality of student records. Students' records are kept in separate files with access by appropriate personnel only. The Disabilities Services office cannot share the information about the student's disability with anyone unless requested by the student. Personal information shared between the DSS service provider and the student will not be shared with anyone either, including the parents, unless the student has specifically requested the information to be shared.

Choosing to disclose about an autism spectrum disorder to other students or to instructors can be more complicated than disclosing to Disabilities Services. Disclosing to the DSS office is typically a fairly easy process for the student. A procedure is in place that describes what documents are needed and how and when to present these documents to the Disabilities Services office. The service provider should be familiar with the challenges of the disability and be sensitive to the needs of the student. Other students or instructors, on the other hand, typically would not know much about the autism spectrum and may need more explanation about the individual needs of the student. The student will most likely have to initiate a conversation in order to disclose their needs, and this is something that can be difficult for many students. Students may be concerned that instructors or other students may be unsympathetic or even hostile. Because of the stress of disclosing, some students may choose not to disclose to people outside of Disabilities Services.

In *Towards Success in Tertiary Study with Asperger's Syndrome and Other Autism Spectrum Disorders* (Al-Mahmood *et al.* 1998), a booklet written for students studying in higher education settings in Australia, the authors suggest several advantages of disclosing. In addition to helping students obtain services, disclosing will help the student be understood and accepted and get emotional support if needed. Disclosing may also lead to instructors showing more interest in the student and make it easier for them to be supportive in difficult situations. If a student discloses about their disability it can also prevent them from being discriminated against because of that disability (Al-Mahmood *et al.* 1998).

A student's decision to self-disclose is similar to the decisions we make as parents when our children are younger. Most parents struggle with the decisions of whom to tell about the diagnosis and how to tell them. Do you tell the parent of your child's playmate in the neighbor-hood? Do you tell the barber, or the soccer coach, or the swimming instructor? Parents make the decision to disclose based on each situation. Will it help the child? Does the individual need to know? The student in college may also need to look at each situation separately and make the decision to disclose based on the need to know. Parents can remind students that they don't have to decide between telling everyone and telling no one. They can choose whom they want to tell and what they tell them.

In Liane Holliday Willey's book, *Pretending to be Normal* (1999), she includes a wonderful appendix entitled "Explaining Who You Are to Those Who Care." She describes some of the benefits of disclosing as well as the risks involved. When deciding whom to tell and whom not to tell, Ms. Willey suggests thinking of people in two groups: those who need to know and those who might not need to know. She believes that those who need to know include individuals who have authority over your actions or your future (teachers, employers, coaches, police officers), people with whom you have strong personal relationships (romantic interests, close friends, relatives, roommates, co-workers) and people to whom you turn for support or advice (religious leaders, counselors, social workers, physicians) (Holliday Willey 1999).

Deciding who doesn't need to know is not often as clear. If a student on the autism spectrum is in a large class with hundreds of students in an auditorium, sharing information about their disability to that particular instructor may not be beneficial. The class may be so large that personal communication between the instructor and the student cannot easily occur. If the course is going to be especially challenging for the student or involve more student participation in class, disclosure may be more important. Courses in sociology, psychology, or communication, while great learning opportunities for a student on the autism spectrum, can be challenging. For these kinds of courses it may be helpful for the student to disclose to the instructor their learning or communication needs.

There are individuals on a college campus who may benefit from knowing about the student's differences. The resident advisor (RA) is someone who will have frequent contact with the student living in the dormitory. If students need help or have a question, the RA will frequently be the first person to whom they turn. The RA may be more supportive and helpful if he or she understands about the student's communication or social difficulties. If the student has a roommate it may be necessary to share information about the autism spectrum with that individual. If the student gets sick and needs to use the health services on campus it may be necessary to disclose the diagnosis to receive appropriate medical care. The career counselor and the academic advisor may also need to know more about the student's needs in order to advise him or her about course selection, internships and future job options. Tutors and counselors, if they are having regular contact with the student, may need to know more about the student's needs to serve them appropriately.

During his first year at college Eric disclosed about his autism only to the Disabilities Services office. The instructors were not told that he had autism. They knew only that he was working with Disabilities Services and that he needed accommodations. The year went fairly well, but could have gone better. The question of disclosing to instructors came up during the summer between Eric's first and second years of college. Eric was scheduled to take a required course called "Interpersonal communication." Just by the name of the course we knew it could be a challenge for someone on the autism spectrum.

Eric had had an experience with an instructor the previous semester that made us think disclosing could help. The course was required for Eric's major and he needed to receive a final grade of at least a C- or better to get credit for taking the course. When Eric got his final grade it was a D+. I suggested Eric write an e-mail to the instructor and ask if there was any extra credit work he could do to bring up his grade. The response from the instructor was very telling. She said that Eric never seemed to be listening during lectures and that he should have come to her and gotten help if he was having trouble in the class. She said Eric didn't seem to be interested in making sure he was getting and understanding the information. After reading this e-mail together, Eric and I agreed that it may have helped this instructor to have more information about Eric's learning style and his disability.

Eric and I talked during that summer about the advantages and disadvantages of telling the instructor of the interpersonal communication course and his other instructors about his autism and the difficulties he has with social and communication skills. Eric agreed that it would help if instructors knew more about him, but he did not want to initiate talking to the instructors about his autism. Eric wanted to write something about his disability that he could hand or mail to the instructors.

Eric's disclosure form is one page long, and although it states at the beginning that Eric has high-functioning autism, it is primarily a description of his learning style. He states the ways his autism affects his learning such as difficulty with taking tests, difficulties with organizing himself and his materials for assignments, and problems in initiating in small group discussions or activities. The disclosure form also lists some strategies that Eric has found helpful. It includes an explanation of the accommodations he qualifies for through Disabilities Services and ways instructors can make things more visual for students who are visual learners. It also states that Eric needs periodic feedback from the instructor. If a student wants help developing their own self-disclosure form they can ask parents, the service provider on campus, or a professional in the community who has worked with the student to help them create the document. Laurie Quartermain, a therapist at Division TEACCH who works with Eric, helped him develop his disclosure form. A copy of Eric's disclosure form is included in Appendix B.

Eric's disclosure form is now sent to each instructor along with the information from Disabilities Services about accommodations he will need that semester. We hope that the instructors read the information, and that if they have questions, they will ask Eric about them when they meet with him at the beginning of the course. I have never been to any of the meetings between Eric and his instructors and Eric does not share much information with me about these meetings. I don't know if Eric receives many questions or how he does in answering them. For those students who might have difficulty responding to questions about their learning needs, parents or the service provider can help the student think of possible questions that might be asked and responses that would be appropriate. When disclosing, it might also be helpful for the student to have developed a definition of the disability that they are comfortable with or a description of how it affects them. Some individuals on the autism spectrum prefer to use business cards describing autism or Asperger Syndrome that can be handed to people who need more explanation.

In thinking about self-disclosure it is important to remind ourselves that all students on the autism spectrum are individuals. Each student's willingness to self-disclose will depend on how comfortable they feel about themselves and their autism or Asperger Syndrome. This comfort level can depend on many factors including how long they have known about their differences and how long they have had an official diagnosis. How they learned about their disability and what experiences they have had in the past with their peers and with people in the community can also be important factors. If they feel the need to disclose, how much they disclose and how they do it should be their decision alone.

8 Positives of the College Experience

The hard work and possible anxiety of preparing for the transition to college life may overwhelm any considerations of the benefits that can come from the college experience. Every student's experience will be different and some students will fail the academics or have a bad experience in college. This is possible for any student, with or without an autism spectrum disorder. However, with advanced planning and preparation, and with the needed supports in place, the college experience for many on the autism spectrum can be a very positive time in their lives.

Despite having some struggles at times during college, the experience overall has been positive for Eric in many ways. Even the mistakes and problems he has encountered have helped him learn more about himself and about life in general. Parents of children on the autism spectrum sometimes tend to judge whether an experience is positive by whether the child merely survived it. I am reminded of the childhood birthday parties where Eric didn't cry, or the school field trips where Eric didn't require any special help, or the family dinners out when we didn't have to leave the restaurant early. These were successes and were counted as positive experiences because nothing bad happened. College has been positive for Eric in more ways than simple survival. He is a better person because of his college experience and has learned more than I could ever have imagined.

The experience of attending college has given Eric the opportunity to be independent in ways he had never been before. Having to make his own decisions and take care of himself has taught him many skills I would not have been able to teach him. He can find his way to places he has never been. He can communicate with people he has never met before to get what he needs. He can make the daily decisions to take care of himself, his hygiene, his diet, and his health. These independence skills that he has learned while in college are wonderful preparation for what he will need to know when he is out of school and on his own. All students on the autism spectrum going to college, whether living at home or living in a dorm, are going to have experiences that can help them develop better independence skills. A student who commutes to campus and lives at home also must be independent in getting to his classes, completing the academics, and communicating with instructors and other students.

The rigidity and routines that individuals on the autism spectrum sometimes develop can at times interfere with their daily lives. Eric has always had routines in most aspects of his life and they have at times limited him from experiencing new things. His years at college have enabled him to relax his routines and become more flexible. He has had to adapt to changes in schedules and deal with unexpected problems. Though often stressful, these experiences have forced him to venture outside his comfort zone. He has learned that life doesn't end when he has to do something new and that sometimes change can add something interesting to his predictable life. This doesn't mean that Eric now loves change and welcomes trying new things. He still prefers to eat the same foods at meals and he still has many of the same routines he has enjoyed for years, but he deals with the unexpected much better.

Any student in college will undoubtedly have to deal with problems occasionally. In many cases the student will have to solve the problem on their own or with very little help. Eric has learned problem-solving skills because he has had to deal with so many different kinds of situations. There has been a constant stream of things that have broken or not worked properly in the dorm room. The air conditioning, the refrigerator, the computer or printer, all have at some point needed fixing. Each situation has been different, requiring a different person to contact for help with the problem. I would never wish any of these situations on Eric because they are stressful for him, but they have been great learning experiences as well. During the first year of college, when problems like these happened, Eric was at a loss for what to do and relied totally on my husband and me to direct him to the solution. Now, if he can't handle the problem completely by himself, he will go to someone on campus for guidance in solving the problem. He makes this decision on his own and knows to whom he should go for help. This indicates an incredible improvement in his problem-solving skills.

In order to solve the everyday problems that have come up in college, Eric has had to become comfortable asking for help. This is a difficult but necessary skill for all students on the autism spectrum. Parents and teachers often spend years trying to teach students not only to recognize when they need help, but to ask appropriately for that help. Eric has been forced to deal with unexpected problems on his own and has learned to report the problem to the correct people, find out why the problem exists, and request help to fix the problem. It is less stressful for him to ask for help now because he has had these experiences.

Eric has also learned to make choices, often a difficult task for someone on the autism spectrum. Having too many choices can be over-whelming. Making a choice between several attractive options can also be difficult for a student. As a college student Eric has many more choices than he ever had when living at home with us. He has to make choices every day of what to wear, what to do during his free time, what to eat, and when to study. The years he has spent at college have helped him be more confident in making these kinds of choices. Eric has strategies now that he uses to help him make choices. If it's a particularly difficult decision for him he knows how to make a list of pros and cons and use that to clarify the advantages of one choice over another. He has also learned from the bad choices he has made and we hope will make better choices in the future.

Everything that happens to the student on the autism spectrum in college can be a learning opportunity. In addition to learning from his mistakes, Eric has learned more about himself from the things he has accomplished. He has developed more self-confidence and better self-esteem. College has helped him realize that he can do things he thought he couldn't and that he can survive experiences that are stressful and learn from them. Parents need to frequently compliment the student for the many things they accomplish daily in college, not just for good grades. Finding a new class on the first day of a semester, attending a meeting, registering successfully for a service, are all reasons for congratulating the student on their effort.

For the last four years, Eric has been a part of a community of his peers and more enveloped in the lifestyle of young people than he ever has been before. This experience has given him insights into how other young adults think, act, dress, and talk. Because students on the autism spectrum often have difficulty "fitting in" with their peers, they can benefit from watching and learning from the actions of those around them. Of course some of the behaviors of fellow students may not be wonderful examples to model. Even the sometimes inappropriate behaviors of his peers have given Eric the opportunity to see that people have different reactions to situations and different perspectives.

Learning is a big part of what college is all about. Where else can someone have the opportunity to learn so much in such a wide variety of subjects? College has helped to broaden Eric's interests. He still enjoys his courses about animals but he now enjoys studying insects as well. He has developed an interest in anthropology that he never had before going to college. He has learned to enjoy fantasy novels after taking a fantasy literature course and learned to bowl from taking a bowling physical education course. He has enjoyed psychology and sociology courses and does quite well in them. These classes and the interpersonal communication class have taught him about people and their behaviors, information that can be especially helpful to someone on the autism spectrum.

Living away from home has helped Eric develop skills needed for taking care of himself, especially when he is sick. One of my biggest concerns when he left for school was that he would get sick and not be able to take adequate care of himself. During the four years he has been at college, Eric has had illnesses and has learned what to do. When he got sick during exams in his freshman year I encouraged Eric to go to student health on campus and see a doctor. I waited patiently to hear from Eric about his doctor's appointment. Eric never called me to report about his visit and when I finally called him he told me that he had pneumonia. Eric didn't understand how concerned I was, didn't know that pneumonia was a serious illness, and didn't realize I would want and need to know that he had pneumonia. This was a good learning experience for Eric because now he knows that pneumonia goes on the list of things parents really need to know about.

The college experience can help students learn more about how to work with the system and the bureaucracy adults frequently have to deal with in life. There are many forms to be signed, registrations to be done, deadlines to meet, and rules to follow in a college setting. Having computer access to many of these processes has decreased the frustrations that go with waiting in lines and waiting on hold on the telephone. Having papers to sign and deadlines to meet has been a good learning experience for Eric to help him prepare for future adult services he will need to access when he is more independent.

Another positive aspect of college is the social opportunities that are available for students. Some students will feel accepted socially in the college setting and will develop friendships and have good experiences with their peers. Other students may struggle socially or may feel depressed and lonely when they do not develop successful interpersonal relationships. Whatever the individual experience of the student on the autism spectrum, college can provide an environment in which to try to improve social skills. College allows students the opportunity to meet and develop relationships with other students with similar interests. Students can choose between many different clubs and support groups that meet on campus. There are also sporting events students can attend. In general, the college environment provides ample opportunities for students to meet other people and to have social experiences with peers.

Eric has never been very social, but despite that he has made a few friends in college. He has a friend from high school who attends the same college and he sees her fairly regularly. There were two girls who came up to him one day on campus and introduced themselves and wanted to make friends. Eric communicates with them off and on by e-mail. A suite mate in his dormitory has invited Eric to watch television in his room a couple of times. Through group projects and class field trips Eric has had opportunities to meet new people. Eric has not initiated many social communications and instead other students have reached out to him. Social experiences are often thrust upon Eric but this has been good because of his difficulty initiating an interaction. College can help students who, like Eric, are not very social become more comfortable in social situations.

There are positive aspects of college for parents as well. Probably most important to me personally is that college has helped me to let go. There is nothing harder than having to back away from involvement in our children's lives. If your son or daughter has a disability, letting go may be even harder. It is scary to give our children the freedom to make mistakes. During the last four years Eric has become more and more independent and my support has been needed less and less. College has allowed me to adjust to letting go of Eric gradually. When he eventually moves out of my home and into a home of his own I believe the adjustment will be easier for me because of our college experience.

College is a learning experience for parents as well as for students. I have learned more about Eric, his interests, his strengths and weaknesses, and his autism. He has surprised me with what he has been able to do and also with what has been difficult for him. He has shown me what is possible and what supports he will need to be independent. I am not as frightened about what his life will be like without me. College has been a test of sorts: a test of survival and an assessment of what Eric will need when he is on his own. In the fairly protected environment of college a student can have the opportunity to show what they can do, to make mistakes, and to experience a greater level of independence. The student's degree of success in this endeavor gives parents and the student information to help set realistic goals for the future.

College has been a good introduction to the world of adult services. After years of learning about services and supports for children with autism, I have entered a new arena where I have to start all over again in finding resources for my now adult son. Through resources on campus, Eric and I have accessed supports and learned about the importance of self-advocacy. In some ways college has been a rehearsal before entering the larger world of adult services outside of the college environment. We have found helpful and knowledgeable individuals within the college setting who can help direct students and parents to other resources in the community.

There have been times over the years as Eric's mother that I have needed someone to remind me of what my son can do. It is hard for me at times to see that Eric doesn't need as much help as I want to give him. I remember the occupational therapist telling me when Eric was three that it was time to potty train him, that he was ready. She was right of course, but I needed someone to tell me. Other professionals over the years have kindly reminded me of Eric's abilities when I didn't see through my need to protect him and help him. College in a way has forced me to give him room to succeed or fail and to be who he is. He has the freedom now to try new things that I would not have encouraged or supported for fear he would fail.

My relationship with my son has grown since he has been in college. Now that we spend time away from each other, we appreciate each other more when we are together. Eric has never been very demonstrative with his affection for others. I have struggled with that over the years but have adjusted to that part of his autism. I know he loves me, but I also know that he has difficulty showing it. Since he has been in college Eric shows more affection to me, from the sound of his voice when I call him to the hugs he gives me when he comes home.

Our relationship has also improved because of the time we have spent together dealing with the problems he has encountered in college. For the first time in our lives we are working together as two adults rather than a mother "fixing" a problem. Eric comes to me for advice, not merely a solution. It's a nice role to have and one I am sure will continue over the years as he becomes more and more independent.

The relationship between Eric and his father has also improved since Eric has been in college. I was always the primary advocate for Eric over the years because I was home and was more available to attend meetings, make phone calls, and transport Eric to his many therapy appointments. Since Eric has been in college he has needed his father's skills and expertise to help fix things or to answer computer-related questions. Eric's father works in the city where the university is located and he has been more accessible to Eric when he needs help. It has been good for their relationship to have Eric need him and appreciate his help.

It is definitely easier to see the positives of college now, four years after Eric's transition to the dorm. It was hard to find much that felt positive at the beginning when I was worried about Eric and missing him. As he struggled at times at college it was not easy for me to see that he was learning from the difficult situations. I had to frequently remind myself over the years that all the experiences, both good and bad, were helping Eric prepare for what comes next in his life.

9 What Comes Next?

I have spent the last 20 years wondering about what will come next for Eric. When he was first diagnosed with autism I began to worry about his future. Like many parents when they first learn their child has a disability, I was immediately afraid of what the future would be like for him. I realized that worrying about his long-term future was not productive and only distracted me from the current issues we were dealing with. I began concentrating my concerns about his future to the near future and what would happen in the next few years. When he was in the third grade, I started worrying about how he was going to do in middle school. In middle school I worried about the transition to high school. My worrying was productive because it helped me focus on planning, preparing Eric, and finding resources. There has always been something ahead of us that was an unknown that needed preparation and work. What comes next after Eric graduates from college is probably the most significant unknown we have had to face.

My dreams for Eric's future were different when he was younger. I was holding on to the dream of the life for him that most resembled my own life—college, a career, marriage, and a family. I still want all these things for him, but I don't expect them. My ideals for a full, rich life may not be a part of Eric's dream for himself. What is most important to me now is that Eric is happy, and I understand that what makes him happy may be different from what I would want for him.

In Temple Grandin and Kate Duffy's book, *Developing Talents: Careers for Individuals with Asperger Syndrome and High-Functioning Autism* (2004), the authors write:

> Parents play the most important role in the task of getting youths on the autism spectrum ready for the job world. If you are the parent of a child on the autism spectrum, help your child cultivate his or her strengths early on. How? By observing and listening and an awful lot of reflection. (p.53)

The authors go on to describe ways parents can nurture these interests and talents and help develop new interests.

When Eric was young I once asked him what he wanted to be when he grew up. He told me he wanted to be a photographer for *National Geographic* magazine. He had never picked up a camera and didn't show any interest in ever learning how to take pictures. After thinking more about why he gave this particular answer, I realized he liked the idea of sitting in a tree watching animals in Africa. I thought at the time that this was a young child's fantasy, like wanting to be a ballerina or a cowboy or a basketball star. Over the years, the interest in photography never developed but the interest in watching animals and learning about them grew. Studying anthropology and zoology has built on this interest and given Eric the motivation he has needed to work hard in his classes in college. I expect this will also be a motivation for him in pursuing a career, I hope in a job that will be connected to animals in some way.

Figuring out how to use this interest and knowledge to build a future career is not easy. Eric will need guidance in finding his career path. He is as he always has been, more focused on the present than the future. He does not think about what will come next after he graduates. My role in this process is to help him understand the decisions he will soon need to make and to help him prepare for what is coming next. I can ask him the questions that will get him thinking about his next decisions. I can remind him of the timeframe he needs to follow in order to accomplish what he decides to do. I can also encourage him and support him as he makes these important decisions.

A career counselor who spoke to parents as part of college orientation stated that employers are looking for an education, not a degree. They are looking for communication skills, team building, work experience, time management skills, and problem-solving skills. All these expectations encompass potentially difficult areas for a student on the autism spectrum. My son may have a degree when he graduates from college, but

I am not confident he will meet this level of expectation from potential employers. Parents may need to help the college student understand the difference between having a degree and having the skills needed to do a job.

In order to set a realistic goal and make a choice for a career, the student has to understand what that choice means. Is it a career that the student has the skills to do? Would the job take place in an environment the student would enjoy? Where will the student have to live to do this job and will transportation be available? Does the job involve people skills and dealing with the public? If so, will this be difficult for the student? All of these issues need to be considered by students as they make their decisions about future employment.

As with every transition in Eric's life I know it will be more successful with preparation and good planning. To help prepare myself I have been researching information about the world of adult services for individuals with disabilities. It is very intimidating dealing with this new world. There are new departments and agencies, different rules and definitions, and complicated processes to go through. When Eric was young I went through a similar learning process, reading everything, making calls, attending workshops. I wanted to know what was available and didn't want to miss any opportunities that would help Eric. It is similar now as I try to learn more about Vocational Rehabilitation, Social Security, supported employment, and residential services. There are new acronyms to learn, new people to educate, and a mountain of paperwork to complete.

Working with adult service providers can be very confusing because of all the documentation required and the numerous people to contact. It is important for the student and parents to keep careful records of which organizations have been contacted and what information has been gathered. Records should be kept of high school transcripts and evaluations, any on-the-job training reports or work experiences, and letters of recommendation from instructors or previous employers. Notes should also be kept on any agencies that have been contacted, when they were contacted, the name of the contact person, and what was discussed. Files can be developed for each agency and should include notes on meetings, conversations, and any correspondence with the agency. Keeping all this information organized may sound difficult, but it can help make a confusing and sometimes overwhelming process a little more manageable.

During this new learning period of my life, unlike when Eric was three, I am not just educating myself. I must now help educate Eric as well. As an adult he has to understand the system well enough to advocate for himself and to make his own decisions. I want him to understand what he might need, what is available, and how to ask for what he needs. This is a lengthy process and not something he can learn quickly. In addition to reading information or attending seminars or workshops, Eric is learning from his experiences. He is learning about advocating and accessing services through his experiences in college. He is learning in these later years of college about vocational skills and career choices. Each resumé he writes, each meeting he attends, and each interview he has will be a learning experience to help prepare him for this next stage in his life.

As his parent I can help him research options, find information about agencies and services, and find job fairs and people he can contact. I think of myself as Eric's secretary sometimes, giving him the background information for the upcoming important meeting he will be attending. The details, the who, what, and when of planning, are difficult for him and he needs help with organizing all the information. I am trying to not make decisions for him but instead to give him the information to make his own decisions. It is similar to his first few semesters of college when he needed more of my support. After several years as a college student he now requires very little help from me and can solve most of his own problems and make his own decisions. I hope that, as he learns more about this next step in his life after college, he will feel more comfortable being independent and will not need my involvement in the details.

The transition from college to employment is as important as or maybe more important than the transition to college from high school. However, there is very little emphasis on helping students with disabilities through this transition. Although many colleges are working to improve career counseling supports for students with disabilities, most do not have programs specific to this population. The career counseling offices on campus are not typically informed about the special needs of students on the autism spectrum. They may not have the expertise to provide assistance beyond the instruction and guidance they provide to students without disabilities. The staff at the college Disabilities Services office would have more knowledge about the disability but are typically not trained to provide career counseling or job search guidance. This can leave a gap in services that unfortunately these students can fall into. Because of this gap in services, parents may find they need to provide more support or guidance to the student through this transition.

Most colleges and universities offer some degree of career counseling services for their students. Career development programs at colleges are required to provide reasonable accommodations to students with disabilities who want to participate. As with other accommodations in college, the student will have to initiate any discussion about accommodations that are needed. Career development professionals are not allowed to ask the student whether they have a disability. If the student discloses their disability to the career development professional, that person cannot talk to a possible employer about the student's disability unless the student gives them permission to do so.

Eric and I are learning together about the career counseling services offered at his university. His university's career center can assess the student's skills and experiences that they can bring to a job. They also help students write resumés and prepare for interviews. The career center offers classes and training opportunities in these areas and can work with students individually if needed. Eric's university has a staff person within the career center who is available to work with those students who have disabilities and are interested in career counseling. She informs the Disabilities Services office about upcoming career training opportunities, internships, and job fairs. This information is then sent by Disabilities Services to the students who receive their services. It is totally up to the student whether or not they take advantage of these opportunities. Parents may want to remind the student about the resources available through the career counseling office and encourage them to contact someone within that office before they graduate from college.

The earlier a student starts exploring career options, the more options they may have for work-based learning experiences such as internships and cooperative education opportunities (co-op). Work-based learning experiences can be extremely important for students with disabilities in college. Students learn more about the work environment and about themselves during an internship. They can "try out" a particular career choice and see if it is a good fit. They can apply skills they have learned in the classroom. The employer can also learn more about the student and how they fit into the workplace. In an internship or a co-op experience there may be fewer expectations on the student than in post-college employment. It is expected to be a learning opportunity and employers are typically more accepting of mistakes. Networking with potential employers can also benefit the student. Many internships or co-op programs can lead to permanent employment following graduation. Work-based learning experiences also give students with disabilities the opportunity to learn what accommodations they may need in the work setting and how to disclose and discuss their disability.

Students can begin looking and planning ahead for a career as early as the freshman year of college. They can start exploring different courses and areas of study to discover their interests and their strengths. They can also start collecting samples of their work for a portfolio if it's appropriate for the field they wish to enter. During the freshman and sophomore years the student begins to get to know their academic advisor, someone who can be an important resource in learning more about a career and what academic requirements are needed. Early in the college years a student can begin researching careers by looking at the various websites of different departments at the college that give descriptions of majors and careers. They can also join professional societies or clubs related to their possible career.

In the summers during the college years students can help build their experiences by working or volunteering in jobs related to their career choice. Any experience, volunteer or paid, will add to their resumé and make useful connections within the field. Eric has had paid and volunteer summer jobs related to his interest in animals. He worked in the animal department at a local museum and worked for a wildlife rehabilitation facility. He enjoyed these experiences and it helped him learn more about what working in this area involves. He also met people in the field who may be good references and resources for future employment.

In the junior year of college the student typically focuses more on the courses within their major. The student will often begin to develop a certain area of interest within the major and can narrow their career choices. During this school year the student should develop their resumé and attend any career fairs that are available. If graduate school is a possibility, the student will need to start investigating that option. In the senior year of college the student should prepare for job interviews, refine their resumé, and attend any employer information sessions or career fairs that are appropriate. Many colleges will offer seminars or workshops related to interviewing skills. These may be particularly helpful for the student on the autism spectrum. Many colleges will also have a service to help students get their resumé out to potential employers. Students should explore what services of this type their college offers.

Many colleges conduct career fairs on campus for students who are looking for internship opportunities or are looking for postgraduate work. Representatives from the federal government, state government, and large and small businesses in the area may be in attendance. The career counselor can help the student prepare for these fairs. They can help the student prepare their resumé or instruct them in interviewing skills. The student needs to keep in regular contact with the career counseling office to find out when these fairs will take place.

Preparing for employment or an internship involves knowing what you want to do. Some internships or jobs may be related to what the student enjoys but may not exactly fit their career goal. A student on the autism spectrum may need some guidance in understanding that their "perfect" job may not be available. It may be necessary to work in a related area and gain needed experience before being able to get the job they would really like to have. Some parents have spoken to me about students on the autism spectrum having unrealistic expectations for a career. Either the career is so specialized that the possibility of getting employment in that area is next to impossible, or the student does not have the necessary skills to be competitive for the career. This is a difficult situation to be in for the student and for the parent. How do parents help the student understand the reality of the situation without damaging their self-esteem?

Students need to evaluate their strengths and weaknesses. With the help of a career counselor, a support person with Disabilities Services, or the parents, the student can explore what they do well and enjoy and what is challenging to them. The student can then look at the requirements of the career they are considering and research the skills that are necessary for that job. This process may clarify for the student what are realistic expectations and also what areas they may need to work on to gain the skills they will need. The student may discover a focus they should pursue within their career that builds on their strengths. Whatever is learned from this experience will help the student better understand themselves and what makes them happy.

A friend of mine has a son on the autism spectrum who is in college. She has described how she and her husband have helped their son clarify what choices he may have after college. The family had a meeting to talk about the student's future. Each participant in the meeting, including the student, brought up two issues they were concerned about or wanted to prepare for related to the student's life after college. Some of the issues that came up included health insurance, where the student would live, and possible long-term career choices. It was a productive opportunity for each participant to address questions about the future and set goals and steps to reach these goals. This kind of family meeting may be a good idea to open a dialogue about the student's future.

As the college student prepares to begin job hunting it is important that they are aware of their legal rights related to employment. The Americans with Disabilities Act (ADA) applies to employment rights as well as the educational rights of students with disabilities. The ADA requires that an employer provide reasonable accommodations that will allow the employee to perform the essential functions of a job. Reasonable accommodations can include modifying equipment, schedules or training materials, restructuring a job, providing an interpreter, and making the workplace physically accessible. Employers may not discriminate against an individual who has a disability and who is qualified to perform a job. Employers may not ask about a disability or medical condition during the interview process. They can only ask the applicant about specific job skills needed for the position. The employer also cannot require the applicant to take a medical exam before making a job offer (U.S. Equal Employment Opportunity Commission 1997).

The employer is not required to make reasonable accommodations for an employee if the employer is not aware of the disability. Some disabilities, such as autism spectrum disorders, are not physically obvious. In this situation, the need for an accommodation will have to be initiated by the employee. This brings up a very important issue: whether the individual with a disability should tell their employer about their disability. Determining the need to disclose in employment is similar to making the decision to disclose in the educational setting. In college, if the student needs accommodations to be successful academically, they need to disclose to receive accommodations. If the individual thinks they will need a reasonable accommodation to perform a job successfully, they should inform the employer of the disability and that an accommodation is needed.

A college student who has a disability and is pursuing a job should carefully consider the issue of disclosure. The student will need to explore their feelings about their disability and weigh the benefits and risks of disclosure. They should think about the particular job and whether they can successfully do the job without accommodations. They also need to ask themselves whether the disability is going to be obvious to the employer or co-workers. If the student decides not to disclose, they should make sure they can do the essential functions of the job before they accept the position. If the student decides to disclose, they will need to plan in advance how they will do so. They have to think about who they will disclose to, what they will say, and when they will disclose.

If the student decides to disclose their disability there are different options as to when they can disclose to an employer. If the student discloses on their resumé or on a job application they could be disqualified before they have the chance to defend their strengths and skills. In this situation the employer gets to decide whether the disability is an issue before even meeting and talking to the student. Although this option may make it harder for the student to find work, when the student does find a job they will know that the employer is accepting of the disability.

Some students decide to disclose during the initial interview for a job. This may show the employer that the individual is honest and forthcoming and it gives the employer and the student the opportunity to discuss the disability openly. However, this can also put a great deal of stress on the student, who will need to know how to describe the disability in an understandable, positive way. Disclosing during the job interview can also put emphasis on the disability rather than the skills and qualifications of the applicant.

If the student doesn't disclose during the interview and it goes well, they may consider disclosing at the time of the job offer. The student is being honest to the employer, and if the student will need any accommodations on the job disclosing might be appropriate at this time. Chances are the employer already feels that the student has the skills for the job or they wouldn't be making a job offer. The employer, one hopes, will respect the student's honesty in disclosing the disability.

If a student decides not to disclose until after starting work, they get the opportunity to prove themselves on the job. If they decide to disclose later or a problem develops that leads to disclosure, the employer may resent not knowing sooner. They may feel they should have been told before the hiring decision was made. There are obviously many factors to consider and the decision about disclosing is not an easy one.

I am not sure how I feel about the issue of disclosure and employment for my son. I think each possible employment situation has to be looked at separately and evaluated based on the responsibilities of the job, how well Eric is suited to the position, and the personality of the employer. The decision to disclose or not is ultimately Eric's decision. If he asks for my opinion I will talk to him about the pros and cons to disclosing and support whatever decision he makes. If he decides to disclose, we will talk about when would be the best time and how to do it. It will probably be stressful for Eric to talk about his disability to an employer and he may need to write down or rehearse what he wants to say.

My personal feeling is that Eric's differences will be fairly obvious and disclosing will be appropriate. I am not sure he will have the grades and experience to be competitive with other students graduating with the same degree and competing for the same jobs. I think Eric will need to be in a work environment that will accept him for who he is and respect his strengths and weaknesses. If the employer and people in the workplace are aware of his disability, I feel they will be more accepting. My hope is that Eric will be employed by the museum in our city where he has volunteered for so many years. He loves the environment and feels comfortable there. The people at the museum who know him and have worked with him are very supportive and understand his disability.

To be honest, I didn't have very high expectations of Eric getting a college education that would create a "career" for him. I wanted him to experience college and, if he could handle the academics, graduate. I also wanted him to develop the independence skills he would need to attend college and live in a dormitory. I didn't think very much beyond that. I knew going to college would strengthen his resumé and give him a better chance of getting a job. I also thought it would help future employers understand how capable Eric is when they learn he has a disability and also a college degree.

I believe that finding someone willing to give my son a chance is the key. I know that individuals on the autism spectrum can be wonderful employees, dependable, hard-working, and devoted. They may at times need some support and understanding of their differences, but what they can offer is worth the extra effort.

That future I was anxious about when Eric was first diagnosed is here. I still don't have all the answers and I continue to worry about what comes next. I don't know what Eric will be doing after college, where he will be living, or what he will need. It's scary not knowing. I want to have the answers to all the questions about what comes next, but I don't. College has given Eric an incredible opportunity to grow and learn and, I hope, to improve his odds of being successful in life. The college experience has also taught me a lot about myself, about my son, and about letting go.

We have realized the college dream together, Eric and I, and now we will move to the next stage. The only thing I know is what I hope for my son. I hope for him to have a job he likes, working with people who like him. I hope he will be able to live independently and have friends and social opportunities that enrich his life. I am hopeful that someone will see his potential and be willing to take a chance. These things may not happen right away after college but that's OK. We will continue to do what we have always done: prepare and plan for changes, work on areas of need, build on strengths, and always respect Eric as an individual with his own perspective and choices.

Appendix A Useful Books and Websites

Books

Aquamarine Blue 5: Personal Stories of College Students with Autism edited by Dawn Prince-Hughes (2002) Athens, OH: Ohio University Press.
This is a collection of essays written by college students with Asperger Syndrome and high-functioning autism.

Ask and Tell: Self-Advocacy and Disclosure for People on the Autism Spectrum edited by Stephen M. Shore (2004) Shawnee Mission, KA: Autism Asperger Publishing Company.
This book is written for individuals with Asperger Syndrome and high-functioning autism and addresses the issues of self-advocacy and disclosure as strategies for attaining a constructive and satisfying life.

Asperger Syndrome Employment Workbook: An Employment Workbook for Adults with Asperger Syndrome by Roger N. Meyer (2001) London: Jessica Kingsley Publishers.
A practical guide created to help individuals with Asperger Syndrome and high-functioning autism assess their purpose as working individuals.

Asperger Syndrome in the Family: Redefining Normal by Liane Holliday Willey (2001) London: Jessica Kingsley Publishers.
In her first book, *Pretending to Be Normal: Living with Asperger's Syndrome*, the author described what it was like to grow up with Asperger Syndrome (see below). In this follow-up volume, the author discusses what it is like to be a wife and mother with AS (her youngest daughter also has AS).

Beyond the Wall: Personal Experiences with Autism and Asperger Syndrome by Stephen Shore (2003) Shawnee Mission, KA: Autism Asperger Publishing Company.
The author, who has Asperger Syndrome, offers an autobiographical account of what it is like to live with the disorder.

The Curious Incident of the Dog in the Night-Time by Mark Haddon (2003) New York: Vintage Books.
This is a novel narrated by a 15-year-old teenager with high-functioning autism. The book gives the reader insight into the mind of a person on the autism spectrum.

Developing Talents: Careers for Individuals with Asperger Syndrome and High-Functioning Autism by Temple Grandin and Kate Duffy (2004) Shawnee Mission, KA: Autism Asperger Publishing Company.
Describes unique work challenges for persons with AS and HFA and particular emphasis is placed on developing social skills, modulating emotions, and dealing with sensory issues.

Don't Tell Me What to Do, Just Send Money—The Essential Parenting Guide to the College Years by H.E. Johnson and S. Schelhas-Miller, S. (2000) New York: St. Martin's Press.
This is a comprehensive guide that covers fundamental college issues such as how to prepare for college, adjusting socially, handling crises, and postgraduate choices.

Emergence: Labeled Autistic by Temple Grandin and Margaret M. Scariano (1996) New York, NY: Warner Books.
A first-person portrayal of what it is like to experience autism spectrum disorder. The author, now a well-known scientist and speaker, recounts her memories as a child and young adult with ASD.

Employment for Individuals with Asperger Syndrome or Non-Verbal Learning Disability: Stories and Strategies by Yvona Fast (2004) London: Jessica Kingsley Publishers.
Comprehensive handbook that addresses a variety of key employment issues that will help individuals with AS or NLD find and maintain successful careers.

High-Functioning Individuals with Autism edited by Eric Schopler, Ph.D. and Gary Mesibov, Ph.D. (1992) New York: Plenum Press.
Based on a Division TEACCH annual conference, this book discusses the unique challenges of individuals with high-functioning autism.

How to Choose a College: Guide for the Student with a Disability by J. Jarrow *et al.* (1997) Washington, DC: The American Council on Education and HEATH Resource Center.
A joint project of the Association on Higher Education and Disability and the HEATH Resource Center, this booklet was written to give students with a disability an organized approach to making the decision about college.

How to Find Work that Works for People with Asperger Syndrome: The Ultimate Guide for Getting People with Asperger Syndrome into the Workplace (and keeping them there!) by Gail Hawkins (2004) London: Jessica Kingsley Publishers.
This book was written primarily for family members and professionals who want to help individuals with Asperger Syndrome find meaningful employment.

K & W Guide to Colleges for Students with Learning Disabilities or Attention Deficit Disorder: A Resource Book for Students, Parents and Professionals by Imy F. Wax and Mary Beth Kravets, Seventh Edition (2003) New York: Princeton Review.
A book that helps families seek out the right school for the student's specific needs.

Kaplan Test Prep and Admissions Courses. Books, computer software for preparing for college entrance exams. www.kaptest.com.

Learning How to Learn: Getting Into and Surviving College When You Have a Learning Disability by Joyanne Cobb (2001) Washington, DC: CWLA Press.
This book is written for high school and college students with learning disabilities. It steers students through the process of applying to college, selecting the right classes, and succeeding academically.

Life Behind Glass: A Personal Account of Autistic Spectrum Disorder by Wendy Lawson (1998) London: Jessica Kingsley Publishers.
The author offers a very personal view of life on the autism spectrum.

The Parent's Crash Course in Career Planning: Helping Your College Student Succeed by M.B. Harris and S.L. Jones (1996) Chicago, IL: VGM Career Horizons.
A book that helps parents and the student find workable solutions to major career-planning issues.

Peterson's Colleges with Programs for Students with Learning Disabilities or Attention Deficit Disorders by Peterson's Guides and Stephen S. Strichart (2000) Lawrenceville, NJ: Peterson's.
This book lists more than 750 college programs in the U.S. and Canada for special needs students.

Pretending to be Normal: Living with Asperger's Syndrome by Liane Holliday Willey (1999) London: Jessica Kingsley Publishers.
The author, who has Asperger Syndrome, has written this autobiography to illustrate what it is like to live with AS in different phases of life. The author describes her childhood and college years, including her social struggles and problems with sensory perception.

Special Teaching in Higher Education: Successful Strategies for Access and Inclusion edited by Stuart Powell (2003) London: Kogan Page, Ltd.
This book covers a variety of disabilities and includes a chapter entitled "Students with Autism and Asperger's Syndrome" by Tim Luckett and Stuart Powell.

Succeeding in College with Asperger Syndrome: A Student Guide by John Harpur, Maria Lawlor, and Michael Fitzgerald (2004) London: Jessica Kingsley Publishers.
A book written to help students with Asperger Syndrome meet the challenges of college life. This is a comprehensive handbook that addresses a wide range of important and complex issues, ranging from academics to interactions with the opposite sex.

Thinking in Pictures: And Other Reports from My Life with Autism by Temple Grandin (1995) New York: Vintage Books.
This is the author's second book. She tells the story of what it is like to live with an autism spectrum disorder.

When Kids Go to College: A Parent's Guide to Changing Relationships by B.M. Newman and P.R. Newman (1992) Columbus, OH: Ohio State University Press.
This book describes the changing parent—child relationship and the intellectual, social, and emotional growth that occurs during the college years.

Support, information and resources

Asperger's Syndrome Support Network

Australian-based page.

http://home.vicnet.net.au/~asperger

Asperger Syndrome Education Network, Inc. (ASPEN)

Non-profit organization with its headquarters in New Jersey, USA. Provides education and support to families and individuals affected by autism spectrum disorders.

http://www.aspennj.org/

Association on Higher Education and Disability (AHEAD)

Addresses the needs of individuals with disabilities in higher education.

http://www.ahead.org/

Autism Network International

Self-advocacy organization for people on the autism spectrum.

http://ani.autistics.org/

Autism Society of America

Articles on autism, educational and treatment approaches, and lists of resources.

http://www.autism-society.org/

Autism Society of North Carolina (ASNC)

Information about the autism spectrum and large bookstore on autism-related topics.

http://www.autismsociety-nc.org/

Autistics.org

Resources by and for people on the autism spectrum.

http://www.autistics.org/

College Admissions Testing for Students with Disabilities

Information for students, parents, and educators.

http://www.collegeboard.com/disable/counsel/html/indx000.html

College Internship Program—Berkshire Center

Postsecondary program for young adults with learning differences in Lee, Massachusetts.

http://www.berkshirecenter.org/

College Internship Program—Brevard Center

Postsecondary program for young adults with Asperger Syndrome and nonverbal learning differences in Melbourne, Florida.

http://www.brevardcenter.org/

College Interview Preparation Form

Form to help prepare high school students with learning disabilities for college interviews.

http://www.ldonline.org/ld_indepth/postsecondary/nacac_form2.html

College Parents of America

Includes parent resource center for current and future parents of college students.

http://www.collegeparents.org/

College Planning for Students with Learning Disabilities

Article on college planning including how to develop an appropriate IEP, skills needed in college, and questions to ask about support programs.

http://www.ldonline.org/ld_indepth/postsecondary/eric_collegeplanning.html

College Preparations for Students with High-Functioning Autism

Strategies for students with high-functioning autism or Asperger Syndrome to prepare for college: motivation to work on needed courses, using strengths to compensate for weaknesses, and preparing for standardized tests. Also includes strategies for succeeding once in college.

http://www.professorsadvice.com/

College: You Can Do It!

Publication and video on advice for success in college.

http://www.washington.edu/doit/Video/college.html

Coping: A Survival Guide for People with Asperger's Syndrome

Book on the web written by Marc Segar, a man with Asperger Syndrome.

http://www-users.cs.york.ac.uk/~alistair/survival/

Coulter Video

Videos on transition to college and work, college prep portfolio.

http://www.coultervideo.com

Disabilities, Opportunities, Internetworking and Technology (DO-IT)

Provides mentoring and career information for students with disabilities, and works to increase the number of college students with disabilities in internships and other work experience programs. Also includes resources for higher education professionals.

http://www.washington.edu/doit/

Disability

Official government site on disability issues and rights in the UK.

http://www.disability.gov.uk

DisabilityInfo.gov

Online access to resources, services, and information available throughout the Federal government.

http://www.disAbility.gov

Disability Services @ UNBC

Disclosure and self-advocacy issues for people with disabilities.

http://www.unbc.ca/disabilities/dismod1.html

EmployAbility

European online careers training package aimed at disabled students and graduates.

http://www.ruralnetuk.org/employability/

Entry Point! American Association for the Advancement of Science (AAAS)

Internship program for college students with disabilities majoring in computer science, engineering, mathematics, or physical science (telephone (202) 326-6649).

http://www.entrypoint.org/

European Services for People with Autism (ESPA)

Colleges for students with Autism Spectrum Disorders in the UK.

http://www.espa.org.uk/

Fast Facts for Faculty—Universal Design for Learning

Ohio State University Partnership Grant that provides strategies for instructors to help students.

http://www.osu.edu/grants/dpg/fastfact/undesign.html

Frequently Asked Questions about Section 504 and Postsecondary Education

Most commonly asked questions concerning ADA and postsecondary institutions.

http://www.pacer.org/text/pride/504.htm

Friends Health Connection

Online one-to-one peer support for individuals with similar health problems.

http://www.friendshealthconnection.org/

HEATH Resource Center at George Washington University

Serves as an information exchange about educational support services, policies, procedures, adaptations, and opportunities in higher education, provides disability technical assistance and a wide range of publications.

www.heath.gwu.edu/

Independent Living on the Autistic Spectrum

Online support group for persons on the autism spectrum.

http://www.inlv.demon.nl/

Job Accommodation Network (JAN)

Toll-free service that assists businesses and individuals with disabilities with questions about accommodations and the Americans with Disabilities Act (telephone (800) 526-7234).

http://www.jan.wvu.edu/

MAAP Services for the Autism and Asperger Syndrome, Inc.
Nonprofit organization dedicated to providing information and advice to families of more advanced individuals with autism, Asperger's Syndrome, and pervasive developmental disorder.

http://www.maapservices.org/

Montgomery College Disability Support Services
Strategies for teaching and accommodating students with disabilities.

http://www.montgomerycollege.edu/Departments/dispsvc/

National Autistic Society (UK)
This site includes information about autism and Asperger Syndrome and about support and services available in the UK.

http://www.nas.org.uk/

National Center on Secondary Education and Transition (NCSET)
Website for professionals and parents supporting transition-aged youth with disabilities. The center coordinates national resources, offers technical assistance, and disseminates information related to secondary education and transition for youth with disabilities.

http://www.ncset.org/

North Carolina State University Disability Services for Students
Information sheet on providing academic visual supports.

http://www.ncsu.edu/provost/offices/affirm_action/dss/faculty_staff/visual_supports.html

OASIS (Online Asperger Syndrome Information and Support)
Articles and resources to help families and professionals and individuals with AS.

http://www.udel.edu/bkirby/asperger

Office of Disability Employment Policy
U.S. Department of Labor/State Liaisons—Information about High School HighTech, the Business Leadership Network, Project EMPLOY (telephone (202) 376-6200).

http://www.dol.gov/odep/

Ooops! Wrong Planet! Syndrome Master Link Page

Encyclopedic index of sites on the net related to the autism spectrum.

http://www.isn.net/~jypsy/autlink.htm

Optimizing the Learning Environment for Students with Disabilities: A Faculty/Staff Guide

Strategies for professors and others working with students with disabilities.

http://www.mc.cc.md.us/Departments/dispsvc/tbl-cnts.htm

Person-Centered Planning Education Site

Cornell University site that provides online self-study courses to learn the basics of person-centered planning.

http://www.ilr.cornell.edu/ped/tsal/pcp

Post Secondary Guide by Parent Advocacy Coalition for Educational Rights (PACER)

Provides recommendations for college preparation and lists, publications, and resource links for parents and students with disabilities.

http://www.pacer.org/tatra/post.htm

Postsecondary Innovative Transition Technology (Post-ITT)

Menu of online guidance activities for high school students with disabilities on self-advocacy, assistive technology, planning and applying to college, accessing disability services and adult human services.

http://www.postitt.org/

Preparing for College: An Online Tutorial

Links to Internet resources for college-bound teens with disabilities. Guides students through a set of preparatory experiences.

http://www.washington.edu/doit/Brochures/Academics/cprep.html

Preparing Your Child for College

Comprehensive guide for parents that provides answers to general questions and information on preparing students academically, financing a college education, and the importance of long-range planning.

http://www.ed.gov/pubs/Prepare/

Rehabilitative Services Administration (RSA)

Oversees programs that help people with disabilities gain employment, such as state Vocational Rehabilitation offices.

http://www.ed.gov/about/offices/list/osers/rsa/index.html

Self-Advocacy for College Students

Article on self-advocacy needs for students with learning disabilities in college.

http://www.ldonline.org/ld_indepth/postsecondary/ncld_selfadv.html

Self-Determination Synthesis Project

Located at the University of North Carolina at Charlotte, this site includes publications, lesson plans, and curricula on self-determination.

http://www.uncc.edu/sdsp

Skill: National Bureau for Students with Disabilities

National charity promoting opportunities for young people and adults with any kind of disability in post-16 education, training and employment across the UK.

http://www.skill.org.uk

The Study Hall

Provides information for SAT preparation, getting into college, ways to improve reading speed, and ways to improve memory skills.

http://www.studyhall.com

Study Skills

Suggestions to help with study skills, time management, test-taking strategies, and note taking.

http://www.d.umn.edu/student/loon/acad/strat/

Transition Coalition

Helpful links to sites on postsecondary education, self-determination, transition, and independent living.

http://www.transitioncoalition.org

University Students with Autism and Asperger's Syndrome Website

Articles and resources and first-person accounts.

http://www.cns.dircon.co.uk/index.html

U.S. Equal Employment Opportunity Commission (EEOC)

Provides enforcement guidance on reasonable accommodation and undue hardship under the Americans with Disabilities Act (telephone (800) 669-4000).

http://www.eeoc.gov/

Virginia Polytechnic Institute and State University (Virginia Tech)

Study skills and self-help information includes time scheduling, note taking, proofreading, and writing papers.

http://www.ucc.vt.edu/stdyhlp.html

WNY Collegiate Consortium of Disability Advocates

Information on various topics related to transition and college services. Includes helpful checklists for students to assess their skills and needs before going to college.

http://www.ccdanet.org/ecp_index.html

Workforce Recruitment Program

Creates a database of screened candidates with disabilities seeking summer and permanent positions; employers may request access to a database of applicants majoring in a variety of fields (telephone (202) 376-6200).

http://www.dol.gov/odep/programs/workforc.htm

Wrightslaw

Information about a student's legal rights in college.

http://www.wrightslaw.com

Appendix B Sample Self-Disclosure Form

Learning Guide for John Doe

My name is John Doe and I am a freshman at Learning University. I am majoring in anthropology. I have a learning disability called high-functioning autism. The Disabilities Services Coordinator, Marsha Smith, is aware of my learning needs but I wanted to share some information with you personally.

High-functioning autism affects my learning abilities in the following ways:

- I have difficulty taking tests. It may take me longer to complete the test.

- Some types of tests are more difficult for me. I do better on multiple-choice exams than on essay questions and other open-ended types of testing.

- Paying attention in class is difficult at times, especially to purely verbal lectures.

- I often have difficulty organizing myself and my materials in order to approach a task.

- I may have difficulty initiating and taking the lead in a small group activity.

- My handwriting may be difficult for others to read.

- I may have difficulty distinguishing between relevant and irrelevant information in a lecture and in my study notes.

- I may feel uncomfortable if others sit too close to me or if I am sitting too close to or too far away from the lecturer.

Some strategies that I have found helpful in my education are:

- extended test-taking time

- a separate setting in which to take a test or exam; somewhere that is quiet

- an instructor conveying abstract concepts in a more concrete manner to help me learn (i.e. referencing textbook page/passages, giving concrete examples, practical application of the concept such as role-playing or a lab assignment, videos and slides)

- having an assigned note taker

- choosing my own seat in class

- working in small groups that have people who are organized and who are willing to take the lead

- teachers who provide clear expectations for assignments to help me stay focused and organized

- meeting with the professor periodically for feedback

- having written feedback in addition to the verbal information.

The best way to contact me is via e-mail at: jdoe@learningunlv.com.

References

AHEAD (Association on Higher Education and Disability) (2004) *Section 504: The Law and Its Impact on Postsecondary Education.* [Brochure] Washington, DC: American Council on Education. Available on http://www.ahead.org/

Al-Mahmood, R., McLean, P., Powell, E. and Ryan, J. (1998) *Towards Success in Tertiary Study with Asperger's Syndrome and Other Autism Spectrum Disorders.* Melbourne, Australia: Victorian Co-operative Projects Higher Education Students with a Disability Committee.

Carlton, P. (1998) "Transitioning into the residence hall." *Postsecondary LD Report,* Fall, 6–7.

College Board (2005) *Services for Students with Disabilities.* Available on http://www.collegeboard.com/ssd/prof/index.html.

College Internship Program—Berkshire Center (2004) Available on http://www.berkshirecenter.org/

College Internship Program—Brevard Center (2004) Available on http://www.brevardcenter.org/

Grandin, T. and Duffy, K. (2004) *Developing Talents: Careers for Individuals with Asperger Syndrome and High-Functioning Autism.* Shawnee Mission, KS: Autism Asperger Publishing Co.

HEATH Resource Center (2003) *Creating Options: A Resource on Financial Aid for Students with Disabilities.* Washington, DC: George Washington University.

Heggie, P. (1999) "A mother's perspective on transitioning." *Postsecondary LD Report,* Spring, 4–5.

Holliday Willey, L. (1999) *Pretending to be Normal: Living with Asperger's Syndrome.* London: Jessica Kingsley Publishers.

IDEA (Individuals with Disabilities Education Act) Public Law 101–476, 20 U.S.C. Chapter 33, 1990.

Kruger, D. (2001) "Road less traveled: The path through post secondary education for students with high functioning autism and Aspergers syndrome." *The MAAP* 2, 19–20.

Minnesota Life College (2003) *Real Skills for Real Life.* Richfield, MN: Minnesota Life College. Available on http://www.minnesotalifecollege.com.

Montgomery College Disability Support Services (2004) *Teaching and Accommodating Students with Disabilities.* Available on http://www.montgomerycollege.edu/Departments/dispsvc/

NCSET (National Center on Secondary Education and Transition) (2004) *Self-determination for Postsecondary Students: Frequently Asked Questions.* Minneapolis, MN: University of Minnesota.

NICHCY (National Information Center for Children and Youth with Disabilities) (1991) "Transition summary." *Options after High School for Youth with Disabilities* 7, 15.

NICHCY (National Information Center for Children and Youth with Disabilities) (1993) "Transition summary." *Transition Services in the IEP 3*, 1, 4–5.

Perner, L. (2002) "Preparing to be nerdy where nerdy can be cool: College planning for the high functioning student with autism." Presentation at the Autism Society of America Annual Conference, July.

Reiser, L. (1995) "Planning for meaningful transition from school to adult life." *Sharing* Sept/Oct, 4–5.

State Vocational Rehabilitation Services Program Fact Sheet (2003) Raleigh, NC: North Carolina Vocational Rehabilitation Services Program.

University of Washington, DO-IT (2004) *Access to the Future: Preparing College Students with Disabilities for Careers.* [Brochure] Available on http://www.washington.edu/doit/Brochures/Careers/future.html.

U.S. Department of Education, Office for Civil Rights (2002) *Students with Disabilities Preparing for Postsecondary Education: Know Your Rights and Responsibilities.* Washington, DC.

U.S. Equal Employment Opportunity Commission (1997) *The Americans with Disabilities Act: Your Employment Rights as an Individual with a Disability.* [Brochure] Washington, DC: Equal Employment Opportunity Commission.

West Virginia Autism Training Center at Marshall University (2004) *The College Program for Students with Higher Functioning Autism.* Huntingdon, WV: Marshall University.

Subject Index

Author Index

AHEAD (Association on Higher Education and Disability) 99–100
Al-Mahmood, R. 129–30

Carlton, P. 90
College Board 47–8
College Internship Program – Berkshire Center 67–8
College Internship Program – Brevard Center 67–8

Duffy, K. 141–2

Grandin, T. 141–2

HEATH Resource Center 70
Heggie, P. 44–5
Holliday Willey, L. 130

IDEA (Individuals with Disabilities Education Act) 39

Kruger, D. 122

Minnesota Life College 68
Montgomery College Disability Support Services 118–19

NCSET (National Center on Secondary Education and Transition) 125–6
NICHCY (National Information Center for Children and Youth with Disabilities 49

Perner, L. 99

Reiser, L. 39, 43

State Vocational Rehabilitation Services Program Fact Sheet 121

U.S. Department of Education, Office for Civil Rights 100–1
U.S. Equal Employment Opportunity Commission 148

West Virginia Autism Training Center at Marshall University 68–9